PRAISE FOR THE PAUL I

'A wholly engrossing and sophisticated spy novel set against a forgotten corner of 20th century history. Fascinating and compelling'—William Boyd, author of *Solo*

'A cross between James Bond and Jason Bourne... carefully researched so the history is credible, even instructive... The action is fast and violent and so is the hero'—*Literary Review*

'A taut and tortured exploration of betrayal on the national, ideological and personal levels simultaneously... A cleverly twisted tale of intrigue and deception, this is a masterly excursion back to the bad old days of the Cold War'—*The Times*

'The immediacy of Duns' writing grabs and suspends the reader in a beautifully realized heartbeat of recent history'—*Kirkus Reviews*

PRAISE FOR *DEAD DROP (CODENAME: HERO* IN THE US*)*

'This excellent book contains lessons that are still valid in the 21st century'—Oleg Gordievsky

'Startling and convincing...an irresistible real-life thriller'—Francis Wheen in *The Mail on Sunday*

A Spy Is Born

*Dennis Wheatley and the Secret Roots
of Ian Fleming's James Bond*

JEREMY DUNS

SKERRY

This edition first published 11 June 2019. The right of Jeremy Duns to be identified as the Author of this work has been asserted in accordance with the Copyright, Designs and Patents Act 1988.

Cover: figure, Getty Images; smoke, Moisemarian.
Design: JJD Productions/Skerry

Jeremy Duns is the author of the Paul Dark series of spy novels and *Dead Drop*, a non-fiction book about Oleg Penkovsky (titled *Codename: Hero* in the US). He lives with his family in the Åland archipelago.

For more information, see www.jeremy-duns.com.

ALSO BY JEREMY DUNS

Free Agent
Song of Treason (also published as Free Country)
The Moscow Option
The Dark Chronicles (omnibus)
Spy Out The Land
Dead Drop (Codename: Hero in the US)

SHORTS

News of Devils
Tradecraft
Rogue Royale
Diamonds in the Rough
Duns on Bond (omnibus)
Cabal
Agent of Influence

Contents

Introduction

A COMMON VIEW of Ian Fleming today is that he was a pulp novelist: that his stories are fun, but not to be taken seriously as literature. No full-length analysis of his work has been published since Kingsley Amis and O.F. Snelling's books in the Sixties. At the same time, it's a cultural commonplace that many of the thriller's most popular conventions originated with James Bond, either in Fleming's work or the films, and that Bond is therefore worth looking at as an originator in the genre.

I think both these views are wrong. I feel Fleming has been unjustly critically neglected and deserves recognition as one of the great writers of popular fiction, the creator of an iconic character whose appeal still burns bright today and who is as worthy of study as Raymond Chandler, Dashiell Hammett, Patricia Highsmith or Georges Simenon. But I don't believe he originated most of the genre conventions it's generally believed that he did—many of them were not merely well-established but hackneyed by the time he used them in his work. I think he was a great thriller-writer for other reasons.

This short book has had a long gestation. In 2005, Ajay Chowdhury was putting together the first issue of a new James Bond magazine, *Kiss Kiss Bang Bang*, and asked me to write about the literary roots of Fleming's debut novel, *Casino Royale*, in advance of the release of the film adaptation starring Daniel Craig. While researching the article, I looked again at the 'usual suspects' from the clubland era, but as I dug more deeply I started to wonder if a thriller-writer who had come after them had not been much more of a significant influence. I first read Dennis Wheatley's spy thrillers as a teenager, but on rereading them thought I sensed something much closer to the Bond novels than John Buchan and Sapper. There was virtually no mention of Wheatley as an influence on Fleming in the previous literature, but rereading him had thrown up several similarities that seemed unmistakeable.

After I wrote that article, *Cold Male*, I started out on a similar one examining *Live and Let Die*, but the magazine folded before it was published. However, my research into Fleming's second novel also threw up striking similarities with Wheatley's books, and I decided the subject warranted closer analysis. This took me a couple of years (Wheatley was very prolific), and I also expanded my reading to other writers in the genre to fill gaps in my research and make sure I wasn't taking unjustified leaps or succumbing to confirmation bias. The result was a much longer essay, *The Secret Origins of James Bond*, which is the basis for this book. Since publication of it on the website Spywise.net in 2010, a domino effect has led to Wheatley becoming much more widely identified as one of Fleming's major influences, including by his current publisher—but that wasn't in the air at all when I started researching this topic.

In the last decade or so, I've edited and added to the Spywise essay, expanding my analysis with more context and research, including digging into newspaper archives and declassified M.I.5 files. I was greatly helped in this by the publication of Phil Baker's wonderful biography of Wheatley, *The Devil Is A Gentleman*, which threw me down many new avenues. This fresh version is over double the length of the previous one; unlike Wheatley, I haven't kept myself working through the night with cigarettes and Champagne, but instead have mainly relied on strong Swedish coffee. I feel this now makes the case as best as I can while also, I hope, providing an interesting look at the development of the British thriller, some of the ways in which intelligence activities fed into the genre in the 20th century, and the intricacies of novel-writing. I hope you enjoy it.

Jeremy Duns
Mariehamn, May 2019

I

The Mind of a Nazi

DURING THE SECOND World War, he worked in the upper echelons of Britain's intelligence establishment, helping to plan ingenious operations against the Nazis. He was one of the most popular thriller-writers of the 20th century, but his literary reputation has faded in recent years, with critics lambasting his novels as xenophobic, sexist fantasies. And he created a suave but ruthless British secret agent who was orphaned at a young age, expelled from his public school, smoked exotic cigarettes, had a scar on his face, bedded beautiful women and repeatedly saved the world from the threats of megalomaniacal villains.

His name? Dennis Wheatley.

Since the death of Ian Fleming in 1964, Kingsley Amis, O.F. Snelling and many other critics following in their footsteps have claimed that James Bond's main literary forebears were characters from the early 20th century usually referred to as 'the clubland heroes'. In 1968, the critic Richard Boston claimed that 'the short step from Bulldog Drummond to Ian Fleming's James Bond consisted in giving the hero a sex life', and this perception has lasted: in the 2006 edition of *The Oxford Companion to English Literature*, Fleming's novels are described as 'updated versions of [William] Le Queux and [John] Buchan designed for the Cold War consumer boom and changed sexual *mores* of the 1950s and 1960s'.[1] But in fact the clubland heroes had already been updated, and given sex lives, at least two decades before James Bond's first appearance. There are several characters, incidents and conventions in Fleming's novels inspired by the above-named writers, but a huge number of thrillers were published between the end of the clubland era in the 1920s and *Casino Royale* in 1953, and the genre evolved in that time. Among these post-clubland writers, Wheatley's influence on Fleming has gone almost entirely overlooked, despite it being much more significant than that of the writers usually cited—and playing a crucial role in the development of James Bond.

★

BORN IN 1897, 11 years before Fleming, Dennis Yates Wheatley fought in the trenches in the First World War before taking over his father's wine business in London. Following the 1929 Stock Market Crash he was bankrupted, and in 1933 embarked on a new career as an author, and soon became a best-seller. Dubbed 'the prince of thriller writers' by the *Times Literary Supplement*, he wrote over 70 books, which have sold over 50 million copies in 28 languages. Today, he is best remembered for his novels dealing with black magic and the occult, but he also wrote straight suspense stories, swashbuckling historical adventures and spy thrillers.

By the time the Second World War began, Wheatley had established himself as one of the country's best-selling writers, counting King George VI as one of his fans.[2] At 42 he was too old to fight, but he desperately wanted to help his country. Thanks to a chance encounter made by his wife, a chauffeur for M.I.5, in May 1940 he was asked to submit ideas to the War Office on how Britain could resist an invasion. Fourteen hours later, having worked through the night, Wheatley produced a 7,000-word essay stuffed with inventive suggestions. He was immediately asked to write another paper, this time from the perspective of the enemy: if he were in the Nazi High Command, how would he go about trying to conquer Britain? Helped along by two hundred cigarettes and three magnums of Champagne, Wheatley worked at 'dynamo speed', and within 48 hours had produced a 15,000-word paper on the topic.[3] Its contents shocked the Chiefs of Staff, as Wheatley recalled with laughter in an interview long after the war:

> "'Wheatley's got the mind of a Nazi," they said, "while we're used to running a war like playing a game of cricket."'[4]

After completing further papers, he was invited to become a member of the London Controlling Section, a seven-man team within the Joint Planning Staff of the

War Cabinet that was responsible for devising deception operations against the Axis powers. He was the only civilian to join it.[5] To celebrate his new position, Wheatley had his tailor create a greatcoat lined with scarlet satin, and persuaded Wilkinson's to design him a couple of swagger sticks concealing 15-inch blades 'as a precaution against trouble in the blackout'.[6]

Wheatley was now in his element, given free rein to exercise his thriller-writer's imagination to help defeat the enemy. He spent his time 'thinking up rumours that would cause alarm and despondency'[7] among Germans as well as helping to plan several deception operations, notably GRAFFHAM and HARDBOILED.

The L.C.S. also oversaw deception operations proposed by other parts of the British intelligence apparatus. In 1943, it approved Operation MINCEMEAT, whereby a corpse was dressed as a major in the Royal Marines and washed ashore in Spain with forged documents indicating that the Allies would invade Greece and Sardinia instead of their real target, Sicily. Wheatley was also involved with Operation COPPERHEAD in 1944, whereby an Australian named Clifton James impersonated Field Marshal Montgomery.[8]

During the war, Wheatley became both a colleague and friend of another well-known writer, albeit of travel books rather than novels: Peter Fleming, who worked on deception planning in India and the Far East, and often collaborated with the London Controlling Section.

Like Wheatley, he was a keen advocate of the use of deception as a weapon, and was sometimes frustrated by the lack of resources assigned to it. 'This is a one-horse show and I am the horse,' he complained in a letter to

Wheatley from India in mid-1942. Fleming felt that what was needed from the L.C.S. was not merely red herrings to mislead the enemy, but 'purple whales'—the phrase was later given as a codename to an operation whereby the Chinese were used to sell false documents (written by Fleming) to the Japanese.[9]

Wheatley described Peter Fleming in his memoir of his wartime intelligence activities, *The Deception Planners*, which was published posthumously:

> 'Unlike many authors of travel books, who turn out to be pale, bespectacled little men, his bronzed, tight-skinned face always gave the impression that he had just returned from an arduous journey across the Mongolian desert or up some little-known tributary of the Amazon. His lithe, sinewy figure, dark eyes and black hair reminded one of a jaguar, until his quiet smile rendered the simile inappropriate. Physically, he was as fit as any troop-leader of Commandos and, in fact, he had been Chief Instructor at the London District Unarmed Combat School before being sent out to initiate deception in the Far East. He was always immaculate in the gold-peaked cap and freshly-pressed tunic of his regiment, the Grenadier Guards. There only one thing I disliked about Peter. He smoked the foulest pipe I ever came within a yard of, and when he used to sit on the edge of my desk puffing at it, I heartily wished him back in the jungle. But we were most fortunate in having such a courageous, intelligent and imaginative man as our colleague for the war against Japan.'[10]

Wheatley also knew Peter's younger brother Ian, who was thinking up his own outlandish ideas for operations over at Naval Intelligence, where he was the influential personal assistant of the Director, Admiral John Godfrey. According to Dennis Wheatley's biographer, Phil Baker, Wheatley and Ian Fleming dined together from time to time—like Fleming, Wheatley was very good at what today would be called 'networking', and during the war often hosted lunches, inviting interesting and influential figures:

> 'Wheatley would lunch them at the Hungaria and he was a good host, with exceptional wine from his own cellars. As well as colleagues and the occasional writer he lunched a host of others including J.C. Masterman (Bill Younger's old tutor, the MI5 man who later wrote *The Double Cross System*), Peter Fleming, Brigadier Colin Gubbins, who scotched Germany's atomic bomb plans with a raid on its deuterium or "heavy water" plant, Ian Fleming, John Slessor, Max Knight and a legion of others, often in groups of four or six; over a hundred and sixty guest lists survive in his papers.'[11]

Wheatley also hosted dinner parties, to which he invited Ian Fleming on at least two occasions: November 10, 1942, and a New Year's Eve party the same year. Both took place at Wheatley's home in Earl's Court. For the November dinner, Fleming was accompanied by Joan Bright, an on-off girlfriend who was also an influential assistant to General Ismay, Churchill's Chief of Staff in the War Cabinet, and so a colleague of Wheatley. She had typed out one of his earliest papers for the L.C.S.[12] The two other guests were Roland Vintras of the Joint Planning Staff and Colin Gubbins, both also heavily involved in the secret world.[13]

We don't know what was discussed on this or the other occasions these two men met, but it seems likely that they would have been intrigued by each other: they were engaged in similar secret work, and had a similar approach to it, both being noted for their ability to concoct ingenious if occasionally overly fanciful ideas. On the evening of November 10, Wheatley would have had good reason to have been pleased: Operation TORCH, the Allies' successful invasion of north Africa two days earlier, had been aided by several deception operations cooked up by the L.C.S. to once again fool the enemy into believing that the real objective had been elsewhere.

Fleming would also have been in a celebratory mood: 30 Assault Unit, the intelligence-gathering commando group under his command ('my Red Indians', as he called them), had just captured the Italians' naval code-books from a villa near Algiers. Wheatley would, one suspects, have been eager to hear the details of that mission, as it was both a success story related to his own work with TORCH and just the kind of daring escapade that featured in his thrillers—despite his day job, he had published seven novels since the start of the war.

Fleming and Wheatley had a lot else in common. Both appreciated the finer things in life: Wheatley liked to savour elaborate meals, and often followed them with his favourite cigarettes, a Turkish mixture made by Sullivans in the Burlington Arcade. Fleming preferred a Turkish and Balkan mixture by a rival tobacconist, Morlands, who were based in Grosvenor Street—in 1944, one of his girlfriends was killed in a German bombing raid a few hours after collecting two hundred cigarettes for him from the shop.[14]

Wheatley and Fleming also shared a boyish delight in gadgets and weaponry: Wheatley had his special swagger sticks from Wilkinson's, Fleming a small commando dagger made by the same company that he carried with him on foreign assignments. Both men were keen book collectors, and relied on a mutual friend, the antiquarian dealer Percy Muir, to suggest suitable investments.

Wheatley was also friends with Maxwell Knight, who headed M.I.5's countersubversion section and had some eccentric tendencies: he kept a host of animals in his home, and would sometimes be seen taking his pet bear Bessie for a stroll around the streets of Chelsea.[15] However, there's no credible evidence that Fleming knew Knight, and the oft-repeated idea that the two of them, along with Wheatley and the occultist Aleister Crowley, were involved in luring Rudolf Hess to Britain in 1941 stems from a fabrication by serial hoaxer Donald McCormick. Fleming did approach Crowley about trying to influence Hess *after* his arrival in Scotland, but nothing came of that.[16]

Wheatley did know Crowley, having been introduced to him in 1934 by his friend and neighbour Tom Driberg, a journalist who became one of Knight's agents, codenamed M/8; he later became a Labour MP, was compromised by the K.G.B., and became a Soviet asset.[17] Wheatley became fascinated by Crowley, and used him as the basis for two of his villains: Mocata, the black magician in 1935's *The Devil Rides Out* (later played in the film adaptation by Charles Gray opposite Fleming's cousin, Christopher Lee); and Sean O'Kieff, an occultist with 'a hard rat-trap of a mouth' in the 1939 novel *The Quest of Julian Day*. We don't know if Fleming read this novel, but one can't help feeling it would have been up his street: Day, a half-Austrian half-British old Etonian with a double-first from Oxford in Oriental Languages, is up against not just O'Kieff but the rest of 'The Big Seven', the men behind a massive criminal organization involved in espionage, blackmail, dope-running, diamond-smuggling and white-slave trafficking.

At any rate, one suspects thrillers would have been uppermost in Ian Fleming's mind while dining with Dennis Wheatley, for he was a long-standing aficionado of the genre, and harboured the ambition of writing 'the spy story to end all spy stories' himself after the war.[18]

Somewhat ironically, his brother Peter beat him to it—in a manner, anyway. *The Sixth Column*, published in 1951, was a light send-up of the books he and Ian had enjoyed since their schooldays at Eton, when they had devoured the works of Sapper and Sax Rohmer. It also seems to have been something of a send-up of Dennis Wheatley. One of the novel's main characters is a former commando, Archie Strume, who has had unexpected success with a thriller based on his war-time experiences, which he has written as 'an antidote against boredom'. Strume is visited by British intelligence, who ask him to use his thriller-writer's brain to think of ways the enemy might try to harm Britain, so that they can take precautions against them. This, of course, is precisely what Wheatley had been asked to do in 1940, and as he was the only thriller-writer to have been asked to carry out such a job, it seems certain that Peter Fleming got the idea from his friend and former deception-planner.

Strume's melodramatic best-seller featured a dashing commando called Colonel Hackforth, who is fond of saying things like: 'Tell the Minister of Defence to have a midget submarine alongside the Harwich customs jetty not later than last light on Tuesday. It's important.' This, too, appears to be a reference to Wheatley, whose secret agent Gregory Sallust behaves in a similar manner. In *The Black Baroness*, published in 1940, Sallust calls his superior from the Netherlands to ask if permission can be obtained for him 'to be taken on board any naval vessel which might be leaving Harwich for Belgian waters'. His boss says he will 'get in touch with the Admiralty at once'.

Peter dedicated his novel to Ian, and it might have been both a nod to their shared love of such thrillers and a spur for the younger brother: a few months after the publication of *The Sixth Column*, he started writing *Casino Royale*. Strangely enough, its protagonist would also resemble Gregory Sallust.

II

Two Traitors

IAN FLEMING WAS an aficionado of thrillers, and his ambition to write his own was informed by decades reading the genre. When he finally sat down to do so, he was keen to update some of its stuffier conventions. In a letter to *The Manchester Guardian* in 1958, he explained how even the name of his hero was intended to move things on:

> 'One of the reasons why I chose the pseudonym of James Bond for my hero rather than, say, Peregrine Maltravers was that I wished him to be unobtrusive. Exotic things would happen to and around him but he would be a neutral figure—an anonymous blunt instrument wielded by a Government Department.'[19]

Nevertheless, there were old-fashioned elements to his work. Fleming was not a plagiarist, but he sometimes used other authors' characters or plot ideas as springboards. When asked in October 1963 what writers had influenced him, he pointed to Dashiell Hammett and Raymond Chandler, adding almost parenthetically:

> 'I suppose, if I were to examine the problem in depth, I'd go back to my childhood and find some roots of interest in E. Phillips Oppenheim and Sax Rohmer. Perhaps they played an important part.'[20]

This is what his brother might have called a 'purple whale'. Hammett and Chandler were influences on his prose style, but they also had great cachet for Fleming, who wanted to be as up-to-date and hard-boiled. Oppenheim and Rohmer were both rather forgotten and fusty English thriller-writers, but their influence on his work was far greater. Rohmer's 'Oriental mastermind' Dr Fu Manchu was the inspiration for Dr Julius No, while Oppenheim's glamorous spies were precursors to his hero in a way Philip Marlowe and Sam Spade never were, as Fleming obliquely acknowledged through Gala Brand's musing about James Bond in *Moonraker*:

> 'Well, at any rate she had put him in his place and shown him that she wasn't impressed by dashing young men from the Secret Service, however romantic they might look. There were just as good-looking men in the Special Branch, and they were real detectives, not just people that Phillips Oppenheim had dreamed up with fast cars and special cigarettes with gold bands on them and shoulder-holsters.'

Oppenheim and Rohmer were nevertheless largely indirect influences, predecessors who had helped establish the formula of the thriller. But Fleming sometimes drew on other authors' work much more extensively, working directly from scenes, adding dozens of new elements and ideas, as well as his own glittering prose style, to transform them into something fresh and new. But the original can sometimes still be seen peeking through.

An example of this can be found in Chapters 5 and 6 of *Thunderball*, in which we are introduced to one of Fleming's most famous villains, Ernst Stavro Blofeld. The opening description of Blofeld, and his effect on others, is modelled on a similar passage in Sapper's first Bulldog Drummond novel, published in 1920. We first meet Sapper's nemesis Carl Peterson at a hotel in Switzerland, where he is in disguise as a French count:

> 'To even the most superficial observer the giver of the feast was a man of power: a man capable of forming instant decisions and of carrying them through...
>
> And if so much was obvious to the superficial observer, it was more than obvious to the three men who stood by the fire watching him. They were what they were simply owing to the fact that they were not superficial servers of humanity; and each one of them, as he watched his host, realised that he was in the presence of a great man.'

In *Thunderball*, Fleming described Blofeld in similar terms, punched up several notches:

> 'Any man seeing No. 2, for that was the chairman's number of the month, even for the first time would have looked at him with some

degree of the same feelings, for he was one of those men—one meets perhaps only two or three in a lifetime—who seem almost to suck the eyes out of your head. These rare men are apt to possess three basic attributes—their physical appearance is extraordinary, they have a quality of relaxation, of inner certainty, and they exude a powerful animal magnetism. The herd has always recognized the other-worldliness of these phenomena and in primitive tribes you will find that any man singled out by nature in this fashion will also have been chosen by the tribe to be their chief. Certain great men of history, perhaps Genghis Khan, Alexander the Great, Napoleon, among the politicians, have had these qualities. Perhaps they even explain the hypnotic sway of an altogether more meagre individual, the otherwise inexplicable Adolf Hitler, over eighty million of the most gifted nation in Europe. Certainly No. 2 had these qualities and any man in the street would have recognized them – let alone these twenty chosen men. For them, despite the deep cynicism ingrained in their respective callings, despite their basic insensitivity towards the human race, he was, however reluctantly, their Supreme Commander—almost their god.'

In both cases, the super-villain is introduced by discussing the effect of his mere presence on others, a decisive force that is noticeable to anyone, but which to his fellow criminals is evidence of a great man or, in Fleming's inflation, makes him almost a god.

But while this passage owed a debt to Sapper, the basic idea and structure of these chapters draws much more directly on a far more obscure source: *The Outlaws of the Air*, a novel by George Griffith published in 1894. Griffith had been a successful author in his day, but by the time Fleming sat down to write *Thunderball* in 1960, basing it partly on his aborted film script with Kevin McClory and others, this book was very obscure. However, in 1957, its opening scene had been extracted in *The Spy's Bedside Book* by Graham Greene and his brother Hugh. Along with work by E Phillips Oppenheim, William Le Queux, Eric Ambler and Graham Greene himself, the anthology also included excerpts from *Casino Royale*, *Moonraker*, and *From Russia, With Love*. Fleming reviewed *The Spy's Bedside Book* in *The Sunday Times* in November 1957, using it to get down some of his own thoughts about the bleak realities of the espionage world that, he argued, too rarely seemed to feature in spy fiction:

> 'Here, it seems to me, is the stuff of a great novel which no one has attempted and whose fringes have been only touched on by Somerset Maugham, Eric Ambler and Graham Greene.
>
> Seduced from the drab truth by the emotive lushness of espionage, most writers of spy fiction (or spy fact for the matter of that) choose the easier and more profitable thriller approach and, with the exception of the three I mention above, it is only the best of the others—Buchan, George Griffith, and O. Henry—who can be reread except as a joke. They do date so terribly, these fairy stories of our teens—their language, their steam-age wars, their moustaches, their exclamation marks! Even their gimmicks lack the high seriousness with which the thriller writer should approach his

subject. One shivered pleasurably at Khokhlov's explosive cigarette lighter, but, surely, even in those days of other smoking habits William Le Queux's explosive cigar which blew the Privy Councillor's face off must have made our fathers chuckle rather than shiver.'[21]

This is a peculiar review in several ways. Fleming had a somewhat conflicted relationship with Graham Greene, and it could be his insistence on 'the high seriousness with which the thriller writer should approach his subject' is mickey-taking, or perhaps a kind of passive-aggressive swipe at Greene editing a collection of excerpts that were largely from the more fantastic end of the spy fiction spectrum, including Fleming's work—he had used Khokhlov's explosive cigarette lighter as inspiration in *From Russia, With Love*. But it's the mention of Griffith that is especially striking in terms of what would follow. It's pretty odd for Fleming to have placed John Buchan in the same category of writer tackling the 'drab truth' of the spy world as Maugham, Ambler and Greene himself, but it is downright bizarre to have also placed in this category O. Henry, a well-known short story writer excerpted in the book but not in any way known as a spy writer, and George Griffith, also excerpted, but a science fiction novelist long out of favour, whose novels had dated and were filled with 'steam-age' wars. Part of the reason the Greenes had included these writers was for the fun of finding spyish bits popping up in unexpected places.

The excerpt they used from Griffith's *The Outlaws of the Air*—which is preceded by one from Peter Fleming's *Invasion 1940*—follows 'the most dangerous man in Europe', Max Renault, through the streets of London as he makes his way to a secret meeting of 'Autonomie Group Number 7', the anarchist terror group he heads. The group's headquarters are in the building of the 'Social Club and Eclectic Institute', all of whose genuine and law-abiding members have long since gone home. As he enters the premises, Renault greets the four men and three women seated around a table, then draws a gun on one of the men, Victor Berthauld, and accuses him of being a traitor:

> 'Berthauld sat for a moment speechless with fear. Then, with an imprecation on his lips, he leapt to his feet. Not a hand was moved to restrain him, but as he rose to his full height, Renault's arm straightened out, there was a crack and a flash, and a little puff of plaster reduced to dust leapt out of the angle of the wall behind him; but before the bullet struck the wall, it had passed through his forehead and out at the back of his head, his body shrank together and collapsed in a huddled heap in his chair, and Max, putting his pistol back into his pocket, said, just as quietly as before:
>
> "It's a curious thing that even among eight of us we must have a traitor. I hope there aren't any more about. Take that thing down to the cellar, and then let us get to business; I've something important to tell you."'[22]

In *Thunderball*, we are taken inside a meeting of the Special Executive for Counterintelligence, Terrorism, Revenge and Extortion at the Paris headquarters of its front organization, the Fraternité Internationale de la Resistance Contre l'Oppression. Unlike Renault, Blofeld deliberately accuses the wrong man first, and the method of execution is different—he is electrocuted in his chair rather than shot.

The corpse is also left in the room rather than being cleared away, which is rather nastier, but the idea of this scene is unmistakeably the same as Griffith's: a terrorist organization meets around a table at its front headquarters and the ruthless leader kills one of the group's member on the spot on suspicion of treason, thereby setting a chilling example for the others. In both scenes, the traitor is a Corsican, which set alongside all the other similarities seems too unusual a choice to be coincidental. What makes it unmistakeable, though, is that Griffith's traitor is named *Berthauld*, while Fleming's is *Borraud*. A Corsican traitor being killed in a scene so similar in conception, with a two-syllable surname starting with the same letter and ending with the same phonetically pronounced syllable is the smoking gun, if needed, that Fleming worked from Griffith. So much so that it seems Fleming was deliberately pointing to it: the name 'Borraud' said in an English accent sounds like 'borrowed', which reads like a dry admission he had borrowed it from Griffith.

That might sound implausible, but there are other examples of Fleming placing markers about his influences in his novels to head off any criticism he had worked too closely from them. A couple of weeks after the release of the first Bond film, *Dr No*, in October 1962, I.T.V. broadcast a programme examining the Fleming phenomenon and putting it into context:

> 'Before Bond came Bulldog Drummond, who saved the country from foreign subversion in a score of "Sapper" novels. He has a DSO from World War I, a lethal straight left, a plus

handicap at golf. He had also had a topping wife called Phyllis who kept getting captured. His principle enemies were Carl and after Carl's death Irma Peterson, but for Drummond all foreigners were suspect, whether Dagos, wops, huns or Russkies.'[23]

It's highly likely that Fleming would have watched this, as it was a nationally broadcast television programme about his work that was also promoting the first film adapted from it. If so, he might well have flinched at the mention of Drummond's nemesis Carl Peterson. At any rate, Fleming decided to embrace the similarity spotted by the programme. In *On Her Majesty's Service*, published in April 1963, he had Blofeld disguise himself as a count, and gave him a partner named Irma. The message was clear: 'Oh, I am well aware of the similarity, thank you, it's a deliberate homage.' Any complaint about the proximity of Blofeld to Peterson in *Thunderball* would now be undercut by the surfeit of even more unmissable similarities in the later novel. I think the mention of Griffith in his *Sunday Times* review of *The Spy's Bedside Book* might have been for similar motives: if any reader were to spot the similarity between these scenes—as Graham Greene might well have done—Fleming would have been able to point out he was simply trying out his own spin on a writer who he had already stated in print he rated as one of the great practitioners of spy fiction.

III

Scars and Girls

ALSO EXCERPTED IN *The Spy's Bedside Book* was Dennis Wheatley's short story *Espionage*, featuring a showdown in a bathroom at the Paris Ritz, and it was to Wheatley's work that Fleming would most often return, particularly his character Gregory Sallust. Sallust first appeared in 1934 in *Black August*, a bleak tale set in an undated future in which Britain is rapidly descending into anarchy. Advance copies sent to libraries and booksellers led to so many orders that the book had to be reprinted six times before it was even published.

Sallust, the novel's protagonist, is described as 'cruel', 'cynical' and 'fatalistic'. A journalist by profession, he initially appears to be in a similar mould to Leslie Charteris' Saint: a devil-may-care lady-killer with scant respect for the law. His response to the crisis is to hire a general's uniform and commandeer an unwitting platoon to help him make good an escape to the West Indies. But along with the heroics customary for a thriller of the time, Sallust is unusually brutal and cavalier, at one point confessing that while the worsening situation has been hell for many people, he's enjoying it. Facing the prospect of being shot by firing squad towards the close of the book, he quotes Rudyard Kipling's bawdy poem *The Ladies*: 'I've taken my fun where I've found it and now I must pay for my fun.'

Wheatley partly based Sallust on the extravagantly named Gordon Eric Gordon-Tombe, a charismatic officer he had met during the First World War who became a petty criminal and fraudster and was murdered in an infamous case that Wheatley was a little too involved in for his own comfort. Another inspiration was Sapper's Bulldog Drummond—we learn that a scar on his 'lean, rather wolfish face' is a result of a blow received during his night-time excursions across the trenches in the First World War; Drummond famously favoured precisely the same sort of expedition. Wheatley once tried his hand at writing an outline for a Drummond story, which survives.[24]

The following year, Wheatley tried another tack, with a new protagonist. The hero of *The Eunuch of Stamboul* glories in the ludicrous moniker Swithin Destime, which is about as 'Peregrine Maltravers' as one can imagine. Destime takes the Orient Express to Istanbul, where he soon meets a beautiful Russian bookseller called Tania Vorontzoff. Living under the threat of her invalid mother being deported back to Russia, Tania is forced to work as an agent for the fearsome Kazdim Hari Bekar, a terrifying eunuch and head of the city's secret police. Before long, Destime has uncovered a plot by Islamic fanatics plotting a revolution in Turkey, which if successful could lead to world war. He falls in love with an aristocratic English girl, who chides him that he is in over his head: the gifted amateurs of fiction might always be able to know how to act when faced with such events, she tells him, but in real life you need to know what you're doing.

In the latter stages of the book, Destime is captured by Kazdim and two of his henchmen, and he wonders what the gifted amateurs of fiction would do in his place:

> 'No doubt Bulldog Drummond would grab the two thugs, crack their heads together and carry the twenty-stone Eunuch off on his shoulders as a memento of the occasion. The Saint, he feels, would be more likely to poke the Eunuch in the stomach, grab the pistol of the thug nearest to him and reverse it, before remarking: "Brother, permit me. You are not holding that correctly—it should point the *other* way."
>
> Those were the sorts of things he should be doing, Swithin knew quite well, but as it was, he sat there staring dumbly at the Eunuch, while the great brute placidly lit another cigarette and puffed at it thoughtfully, watching him with that unwinking stare by which a snake fascinates a bird.'

It's an amusing scene that shows how closely Wheatley had studied the genre—but it also fatally undermines his protagonist as a hero. Apart from breaking the fourth wall, in drawing so much attention to the fact that Destime doesn't know what he's doing, we simply hanker for the characters he mentions who do.

The novel sold well nevertheless, and was made into a film released the following year, titled *The Secret of Stamboul* (*The Spy in White* in the US). Now renamed Captain Larry Destime, the hero was played by James Mason in one of his earliest starring roles. Frank Vosper played Kazdim, and the similarity to a Bond villain in the mould of Le Chiffre is unmistakeable. Tania and Destime dine on caviar and champagne when Destime is called away by an urgent telephone call. This is a distraction, as Kadzim then summons Tania to his box—he is slowly revealed from shadow, a bulky bald figure in formalwear with a strangulated but sinister and commanding voice: 'You are dining with an Englishman…'

★

DESPITE THE RELATIVE success of *The Eunuch of Stamboul*, it seems Wheatley realised that he was at his best when he played it straight: the novel had a solid Buchan-style plot, but Swithin Destime was too ineffectual a hero to last for more than one novel. Wheatley had previously written a thriller with a character who combined the bravado and style of The Saint with the physical ruthlessness of Bulldog Drummond, but *Black August* hadn't quite worked for other reasons. Now Wheatley went back to Gregory Sallust and tried again, this time inserting him into the kind of adventure he had just put Swithin Destime through.

Published in 1936 after being serialized in *The Daily Mail*, *Contraband* was in many ways the real start of the Sallust series. Wheatley dedicated the book to a friend who liked 'straight' thrillers', and that's just what it is, following a familiar pattern: a gentleman adventurer reports to an older man in the secret service, and is given a mission to stop a villainous plot that has international implications; he races through glamorous casinos and hotels at home and abroad, using his fists and firearms against assorted henchmen until he is drugged, struck unconscious and captured by the rich, deformed villain, who interrogates and/or tortures him; after learning the full particulars of the villain's plan (usually from the villain himself), he escapes, saves the beautiful woman in the cocktail dress he took a fancy to in the first chapter and assures the safety of the realm.

This had been the formula of British secret service stories since the 19th century, but while all its elements are present in *Contraband*, the tone of the novel is often surprising: casinos and luxury hotels had never before been pervaded with quite such a feverish atmosphere of sweat, fear and danger, and the hero's ethics are, as in *Black August*, unusually ambivalent—he ends his adventure protecting the villain's moll from the law because he has fallen in love with her.

In the first chapter of *Contraband*, titled 'Midnight At The Casino', we are introduced to Gregory Sallust as though for the first time: he has been transformed from his previous incarnation as a journalist in a dystopian future into a secret agent in the here and now, gambling in Deauville ten days before *la grande semaine*. Sallust is about to call it a night when he catches sight of an English aristocrat he recognizes, accompanied by a beautiful woman he does not:

'She must be a *poule*, Gregory decided, but a devilish expensive one. Probably most of the heavy bracelets that loaded down her white arms were fake, but you cannot fake clothes as you can diamonds, and he knew that those simple lines of rich material which rose to cup her well-formed breasts had cost a pretty penny. Besides, she was very beautiful.

A little frown of annoyance wrinkled his forehead, catching at the scar which lifted his left eyebrow until his face took on an almost satanic look. What a pity, he thought, that he was returning to England the following day.'

The line about Sallust's scar giving him an almost satanic look appears, with minor variations, in several novels in the series: it tends to show 'a livid white' against his dark features when he is angry. Like *Contraband*, *Casino Royale* opens with a handsome, world-weary British secret agent gambling late at night in a casino in northern France (the fictional resort of Royale-les-Eaux, which Fleming modelled loosely on Deauville and Le Touquet.[25] In Chapter 8 of *Casino Royale*, we learn that Bond also has a scar on his face, although it runs down his right cheek rather than lifting his left eyebrow. It makes him appear 'faintly piratical' and, along with his comma of black hair and cruel mouth, would become part of Fleming's standard description of the character. In the same chapter, we are given the following description of Vesper Lynd:

'Her dress was of black velvet, simple and yet with the touch of splendour that only half a dozen couturiers in the world can achieve.

There was a thin necklace of diamonds at her throat and a diamond clip in the low vee which just exposed the jutting swell of her breasts. She carried a plain black evening bag, a flat oblong which she now held, her arm akimbo, at her waist. Her jet-black hair hung straight and simply to the final inward curl below the chin.

She looked quite superb and Bond's heart lifted.'

In *Contraband*, the woman who lifts Sallust's heart is Sabine Szenty, a Hungarian who turns out to be part of a smuggling gang (the English aristocrat, Gavin Fortescue, a half-crippled dwarf, being the master-villain). Sabine has 'sleek black hair', a 'fresh and healthy' complexion, and wears 'light make-up'. In *Casino Royale*, we are told that Vesper is 'lightly suntanned' and wears no make-up, except on her mouth.

As well as sharing their taste in women's looks, Bond and Sallust have remarkably similar attitudes to the fairer sex:

'He knew from past experience that he could sweep most women off their feet inside a week with the intense excitement of a hectic, furious, laughing yet determined pursuit, and what magnificent elation could be derived from carrying a rich man's darling off from under his very nose despite her better sense and the rich man's opposition. Gregory had done it before and he would certainly have attempted it in this case if only he had had a few days left to work in.

The more he studied her, between making bets, the more the desire to do so strengthened in his mind. He could never bring himself to be anything more than "uncle-ish" to "nice" girls, however attractive, and he barred respectable married women, except on rare occasions, on practical grounds. The aftermath of broken hearts and tear-stained faces with possible threats of being cited as co-respondent by an injured husband was, he considered, too heavy a price to pay. He preferred, when he took the plunge into an affair, a woman whom he could be reasonably certain was content to play his own game. Nothing too easy—in fact it was essential to his pleasure that she should move in luxurious surroundings and be distinguished of her kind, and so quite inaccessible except to men of personality even if they had the wealth which he did not. Then, when victory was achieved, they could laugh together over their ruses, delight in one another to the full and, when the time came as it surely must, part before satiation; a little sadly, perhaps, but as friends who had enriched life's experience by a few more perfect moments.'

This, despite being written by another writer in 1936, will nevertheless be recognizable to anyone familiar with Ian Fleming's work. It chimes very closely with James Bond's attitudes in *Casino Royale*:

'With most women his manner was a mixture of taciturnity and passion. The lengthy approaches to a seduction bored him almost as much as the subsequent mess of disentanglement. He found something grisly in the inevitability of the pattern of each affair. The conventional parabola—sentiment, the touch of the hand, the kiss, the passionate kiss, the feel of the body, the climax in the bed, then more bed, then less bed, then the boredom, the tears and the final bitterness—was to him shameful and hypocritical. Even more he shunned the *mise en scène* for each of these acts in the play—the meeting at a party, the restaurant, the taxi, his flat, her flat, then the weekend by the sea, then the flats again, then the furtive alibis and the final angry farewell on some doorstep in the rain.'

Published 17 years later, this is more sexually explicit than the passage from *Contraband*, as well as being notably darker, more cynical and better-written. But the core of it is the same, with Sallust's desire to avoid 'the aftermath of broken hearts and tear-stained faces' echoed in Bond's disdain for 'the tears and the final bitterness'. Wheatley's depiction of sex was also notably graphic for the time: he has his hero ponder whether a major character is a high-class prostitute—while desiring her.

After the opening chapters, the plots of *Contraband* and *Casino Royale* diverge considerably, although they share a markedly similar tone. Towards the end of the novel, Sallust urges Sabine to turn King's Evidence. She refuses. 'Then there's only one thing for it,' Sallust replies: 'I've got to get you out of England before the police decide to act':

'That would mean your having to give up your job, no?'

'Oh, to hell with the job! I would have given a lot to be in at the death, when we corner Gavin and the Limper, but that's a bagatelle compared with your safety.'

'Are there not extradition laws so that they could bring me back?'

'There are, but I don't think they would apply them. You see, your having saved Wells and myself makes the police reluctant to prosecute you in any case now. It's only that they're bound to do so by the law if they catch you.'

She nodded thoughtfully. 'Where could we go?'

Gregory stood up and, forgetting the abrasions on his chest and back, stretched himself. He grimaced suddenly and lowered his arms. 'The world's big enough and there are plenty of places where the two of us could lose ourselves very happily for a time.'

This, too, feels familiar. After the end of the mission to bankrupt Le Chiffre in *Casino Royale*, Bond initially desires only to sleep with Vesper and, once the attraction has worn off, gently drop her. If that proved too difficult, he considered taking another assignment abroad or 'which was also in his mind, he could resign and travel to different parts of the world as he had always wanted'. He then decides he wants to marry Vesper instead—only for her to kill herself.

Contraband was a best-seller: it was already in its fifth impression within a month of publication.[26] It added 'spy novelist' to Wheatley's established reputation in other genres. In 1938, he was asked by Hutchinson to edit *A Century of Spy Stories*, part of their highly successful series of anthologies, and in the same year he provided an endorsement for *The Oldest Road*, an old-fashioned spy novel that mixed a Buchan-esque international conspiracy with the occult. Wheatley claimed this was a 'really first-class thriller' that had 'the genuine ring of an adventure actually culled from the annals of our Secret Service'. The novel's author, 'D.G. Waring', was Dorothy Waring, also known by her ex-husband's surname Harnett. She had briefly led the British Fascists, and at the time the novel was published was on the Committee of the Nazi-sympathising group The Link.[27]

The Oldest Road made little impact on the thriller despite Wheatley's endorsement, but the genre was rapidly changing, with newcomers ripping up what had previously been acceptable in it. A few years previously, Wheatley had become friends with Reg Cheyney, a brash East Ender who had turned his hand to several professions, including news editor of the *Sunday Graphic* and private detective. Reg was nearly as dodgy as Wheatley's old friend Gordon Eric Gordon-Tombe and, like Dorothy Waring, had also been involved with the far right: in 1931, he had joined Oswald Mosley's New Party, and was in charge of its 'thug section', known as 'Biff Boys'.[28] He was also a writer. After trying out several pseudonyms, he had settled on Peter Cheyney, under which name he published several newspaper and magazine serials, including stories featuring a Raffles-esque jewel thief called Alonzo MacTavish. Cheyney became increasingly influenced by hard-boiled private eye and detective fiction from the United States—the pulps—and in 1936 found enormous success with his debut novel *This Man Is Dangerous*, featuring a wise-cracking, machine-gun-toting F.B.I. agent called Lemmy Caution. The first page gives a fair idea of its tone:

'Take a look at me. My name's Lemmy
Caution by rights but I got so many aliases that
sometimes I don't know if I'm John Doe or it's
Thursday. In Chicago—the place that smart
guys call Chi just so's you'll know they've read
a detective book written by some punk who
always says he nearly got shot by one of
Capone's cannoneers but didn't quite make the
grade—they used to call me "Two-Time"
because they said it always took two slugs to
stop me, an' in the other place where coppers
go funny colours when they think of me they
call me Toledo.'

This was a million miles from Wheatley's prose style, but
the idea of a hero as brutal, ruthless and even lawless as
the villains he tackled was something new in the British
thriller—and Wheatley noticed. The following year, he
wrote the introduction for Cheyney's second book, a
collection of short stories titled *You Can't Hit A Woman*,
saying he was putting readers 'on to a real good thing'.[29]

IV

Day and Knight

WHEATLEY'S NEXT SPY novel was *The Quest of Julian Day*, published in January 1939. Day's full name is Hugo Julian du Crow Fernhurst, which outdoes even Swithim Destime, but the character is referred to as Julian Day by most. Day is up against 'The Big Seven', a gang led by the occultist Sean O'Kieff. Like Le Chiffre in *Casino Royale*, he condescendingly calls the hero 'my dear boy', apparently one of Crowley's most-used expressions.[30]

The other members of The Big Seven are revealed to be Lord Gavin Fortescue, the deformed aristocrat of *Contraband*; Ismail Zakri Bay, an Egyptian; Inosuki Hayashi ('the Jap'); Azreal Mozinsky, a Polish Jew; Count Emilio Mondragora; and Baron Feldmar von Hentzen. While this sounds very much like a prototypical S.P.E.C.T.R.E., Wheatley was drawing on a long-established fondness in thrillers for sinister organizations like this; they can be found in the work of John Buchan, Sax Rohmer and many earlier writers, among them George Griffith.

With a plot featuring a hunt for treasure in Egypt, *The Quest of Julian Day* is a straightforward, but rather forced, adventure story. Day is a reasonably capable hero, but not an especially interesting one. He's very much a return to the gentlemanly tradition: an old Etonian baronet with a double-first from Oxford in Oriental Languages and an expert fencer, he also has a sweet tooth, continually interrupting his mission to find some pralines to nibble.

Wheatley's fantasies about the espionage world were now being overturned by events in his own life. Maxwell Knight recruited Wheatley's stepson Bill, an undergraduate at Oxford, to spy on potential fifth columnists among his fellow students, and not long afterwards asked Wheatley himself to help out with his work. The same month as the publication of *The Quest of Julian Day*, Knight approached him about a young Austrian woman, Friedericka 'Fritzi' Gaertner. She had divorced her husband, a German Jew, a few years earlier and in 1938 had come to Britain to visit her sister, who had recently married the brother of Stewart Menzies, who was the deputy head of M.I.6.[31] She had offered to work for British intelligence in return for being allowed to stay in the country.

Knight had become convinced Gaertner would make an excellent agent to infiltrate Nazi-sympathising circles for him, but there was a snag. She needed a work permit to avoid being interned as an enemy alien, and 'working for M.I.5' obviously wasn't feasible. Knight's first suggestion had been that she get a cover job as 'a sort of super high-class mannequin'—on meeting her he'd noted that 'there is no doubt whatever about her very considerable personal attractiveness'—but she wasn't keen on the idea.[32] Knight now turned to Wheatley: could he not employ her as his secretary/research assistant?

Wheatley interviewed her and, fairly unsurprisingly, was in favour of taking on the attractive young sister-in-law of the deputy head of M.I.6. He wrote to the Ministry of Labour, assuring them that in employing her he wouldn't be taking work from a British subject; he was planning a new novel set in Central Europe that required a translator with a knowledge of local customs across the region, and he 'should certainly not be able to employ a British subject in this capacity'.[33] Knight was delighted by Wheatley's swift response, and wrote to him to say that 'when you turned your attention to literature the intelligence department lost a great opportunity, though I fear the financial rewards in literature are greater than in the world of intrigue!'[34] Wheatley's role within the L.C.S. was still 18 months away.

If he didn't have a plan for a new book at that point, Fritzi Gaertner might well have given him an idea for one. Wheatley prided himself on his research, but while he had visited Germany in 1919, his knowledge of the country under its current regime was, much the same as everyone else's, gleaned from the newspapers and radio broadcasts, with little hope of improving it from his house in London. Now fate had thrown an intelligent and sympathetic native German-speaker onto his doorstep, giving him the opportunity to get the inside track on a locale few British writers could hope to depict with much authority at this moment: Nazi Germany. Even better than that, Fritzi's close family connection to the uppermost level of British intelligence gave him a *second* inside track most thriller-writers would have killed for. For the next few months, her days were kept busy researching and translating information about leading Nazi figures, giving Wheatley 'invaluable' material for many novels to come as well as background knowledge he would later put to use in his L.C.S. papers. And by night, Fritzi became M.I.5 agent GELATINE, attending cocktail parties and dinners hosted by pro-Nazi groups such as The Link, reporting back to Knight.[35]

While she was doing that, Wheatley was hard at work, writing *Sixty Days To Live*, an adventure in a similar vein to *Black August*, featuring an impending comet hitting the earth and ensuing chaos and martial law. It was published on 24 August 1939, and *The Observer* recommended it as 'homeopathic treatment for crisis tensions'.[36] Nevertheless, it was a flop, probably because the title alone was much too grim in the political climate.[37] Eight days following its publication, Germany invaded Poland, and two days after that, Britain was once again at war.

Wheatley didn't waste any time. While trying to persuade Knight and anyone else who would listen to find him a job in which he could serve, he was feverishly writing his next novel. He already had authentic background material gathered by an Austrian-German M.I.5 agent, and a war to set it in. A story set in Germany now would mean going behind enemy lines, an impossible feat—except perhaps for a secret agent. Another spy story was in order, but a mission into Nazi territory would require someone rougher and tougher than a Swithin Destime or Julian Day. Wheatley decided to return once again to Gregory Sallust. He started writing *The Scarlet Impostor* on September 6 1939, just three days after Britain declared war, and finished it on October 19. It was published on January 7 1940, making it one of the first spy novels to be set during the Second World War.

It's also one of the most exciting thrillers of any era, with Sallust jumping from frying pans into fires at every turn across 172,000 words. In *Contraband*, Sallust had been working in an unofficial capacity for the authorities with the understanding that official backing would be provided if necessary; now British intelligence wants him to make contact with a faction of anti-Nazi generals in Germany, and so he is put on a more formal footing. He's even allotted a number:

> '"In view of the importance of your mission, it's a very special number, too; one which has long been vacant and about which there can be no possible mistake. You are now listed by us as Secret Agent No. 1."
>
> Gregory grinned. "I'm deeply flattered."'

Wheatley dedicated the novel to Maxwell Knight: 'My old friend and fellow author, who has often given me good reason to believe that truth really is stranger than fiction'. Knight had become a thriller-writer in 1934, and had dedicated his second novel, *Gunman's Holiday*, to Wheatley and his wife. A 1986 biography of Knight was subtitled 'The Man Who Was M: The Real-life Spymaster Who Inspired Ian Fleming', although there is little evidence this was the case other than the admittedly striking fact that Knight was known as 'M' within M.I.5. Despite being three years younger than Wheatley, he might have been at least part of the inspiration for Gregory Sallust's white-haired mentor and spymaster, Sir Pellinore Gwaine-Cust. In Arthurian legend, King Pellinore or Pellimore hunts the Questing Beast: Knight was an avid hunter and naturist, later becoming well known as a broadcaster on wildlife, and one obituary described him as 'a sane and more effective version of kind King Pellinore'[38]. Coincidence, perhaps, but it would be fitting for a Knight-like mentor to be the agent-runner sending Wheatley's wish fulfilment figure Sallust on his quests.

★

THERE IS SIGNIFICANTLY more action in *The Scarlet Impostor* than *Contraband*, and Wheatley had to work much harder to make his often-implausible plot developments convince. He did this by supporting the breakneck pacing with a strong degree of verisimilitude regarding the situation in Nazi Germany, thanks to Fritzi Gaertner. One of the novel's main characters is Erika von Epp, a beautiful German whose Jewish lover has been killed by 'the brutalities inflicted on him in the concentration-camp at Dachau'. Dachau and the other Nazi concentration camps were not often discussed in Britain this early in the war, but Gaertner would likely have heard about their horrors in some detail. Like Gaertner, Erika's former lover being Jewish makes her a determined opponent of the Nazi regime, but by the same token her not being currently involved with a Jew means she is able to keep up the pose of being a loyal Nazi in order to gather intelligence for the British.

Providing some relief from the depiction of the horrors taking place inside Germany, the novel also featured Wheatley's usual insider's feel for the finer things in life, given added force by his use of real names. Publishers generally required authors to rename any real-life brands they featured, not wishing to provide free advertising. So E. Phillips Oppenheim's novels featured the Milan Hotel, modelled on the Savoy, and Valentine Williams' characters smoked Melania cigarettes, a non-existent brand that could only be bought at London's non-existent Dionysus Club. In Sax Rohmer's novels, real-life political figures were also disguised, so Hitler became 'Rudolph Adlon' and Mussolini 'Monaghani'. An exception seems to have been cars. Although Leslie Charteris' Saint drove non-existent Furillacs and Hirondels, and Dornford Yates' characters favoured the equally fictional Lowland, many other thriller characters drove Rolls Royces, Daimlers, Mercedes-Benzes and Bentleys. Another exception was EF Hornung's Raffles, who smoked Sullivans, perhaps inspiring Wheatley to do the same (there are several references to Raffles in his novels).

Wheatley took this idea and ran with it—his thrillers were set in the real world, with real people in the midst of real events using real brands. While other writers had dabbled in this sort of 'product placement', with *The Scarlet Impostor* Wheatley became the first to feature it on a grand scale. During the course of his mission, Gregory Sallust smokes Sullivans' Turkish mixture cigarettes, escapes from pursuing Nazis on a twin-cylinder

BMW motorbike and tells a beautiful German aristocrat he hopes to dine with her in the Ritz after the war. He drinks two Bacardis and pineapple juice (his favourite cocktail, we are told), some pre-1914 Mentzendorff Kümmel, a Vermouth Cassis and a few swigs of unspecified brandy, and we learn that his gun is a Mauser automatic and his tailor West's of Savile Row.

Wheatley integrated many of these details into his plot. When Sallust is in danger of being interned in a concentration camp in Holland for the rest of the war, he sends a message to his chief in London that he knows will be intercepted, asking after an 'Otto Mentzendorff'. Sir Pellinore immediately recognises the name of the Kümmel they drank together a few weeks earlier and sends Sallust's former batman Rudd to help him escape. Rudd turns up disguised as an English gent:

> 'He was wearing one of Gregory's smart blue lounge suits with a Sulka tie, Beale and Inman shirt, Scott hat and Lobb shoes—all from Gregory's wardrobe.'

The tie is later revealed to have a hidden compartment, and in a subsequent novel Sallust's Beale and Inman shirt stops him from getting shot after a Russian general checks its label to make sure he's not a Nazi spy. Wheatley used many of these brands himself, and was sprinkling his knowledge into the action to draw readers into a life of luxury, much as he had done when writing catalogues to entice customers as a wine merchant.

Ian Fleming is, of course, famous for using brands in his work in this way. In his 1962 essay *How To Write A*

Thriller, he discussed why such details were irresistible to him:

> 'I'm excited by the poetry of things and places, and the pace of my story sometimes suffers while I take the reader by the throat and stuff him with great gobbets of what I consider should interest him, at the same time shaking him furiously and shouting "Like this, damn you!"'[39]

Later in the same essay, he cites the use of real places and things as one of two devices in which a thriller-writer can bring a reader along even when the plot is wildly improbable:

> 'First, the speed of narrative, which hustles the reader quickly beyond each danger point of mockery and, secondly the constant use of familiar household names and objects which reassure him that he and the writer have still got their feet on the ground. Real names of things come in useful: a Ronson lighter, a 4½ litre Bentley with an Amherst-Villiers super-charger (please note the solid exactitude), the Ritz Hotel in London. All are points to comfort and reassure the reader on his journey into fantastic adventure.'[40]

Fleming, like Wheatley, used this device to reassure readers he still had his feet on the ground, but it was also important that it was rather *special* ground. This entailed more than simply throwing in lots of well-known brands. In *The Scarlet Impostor*, Gregory Sallust keeps his Sullivans cigarettes in a 'plain engine-turned gold case with no monogram or initials'. The simple and unnamed becomes the ultimate brand, its anonymity telling us that this is a man who appreciates a well-crafted object regardless of whether its manufacturer has a reputation. The case is still made of gold, though, and, the crucial telling detail, is 'engine-turned'—there's the solid exactitude. The unadorned case also gives added credibility to the special Turkish mixture cigarettes it contains: Sallust doesn't smoke them for their cachet, but through the same love of good quality. It's pure coincidence that they're so exclusive.

Wheatley used this technique to great effect in *The Scarlet Impostor*. In the second half of the novel, Sallust arrives in Paris searching for members of a Communist anti-Nazi cell:

> 'Whenever he stayed in the French capital he put up at the St Regis, in the Rue Jean Goujon, just off the Champs Elysées. It was a quiet hotel and Gregory preferred it to the larger places, although it was quite as expensive, because each of the rooms was furnished with individual pieces. Many of them were valuable antiques, giving the place the atmosphere of a beautifully furnished private house rather than of an hotel, and Gregory liked luxury and comfort whenever he could get it.'

Moments of luxury and comfort have been mainstays in the lives of fictional secret agents since the birth of the thriller, but Wheatley knew that the devil was in the details, and took the convention much further than previously. After checking into the St Regis, Sallust's mission 'requires' him to woo a beautiful young Frenchwoman, Collette. He's not sure where to take her to dinner. After considering and rejecting the Tour d'Argent, the Café de Paris and Pocardi's for varying reasons, he remembers the Vert Galant, 'down by the river on the right bank':

> 'Quiet and unostentatious, it was yet one of the oldest-established restaurants in Paris, and the cooking there was excellent.'

Collette approves of his choice:

> 'Real French cooking—not the sort of messed-up things they make for you English and the Americans in the smart places—so I have been told. I have never been there and I'd love to go, but I'm afraid you will find it very expensive.'

What's the purpose of this for readers in a fast-paced thriller? We are being shown that Sallust is not simply a man of means (although he is that, too), but that he has a *connoisseur's* tastes—and in 1940 as today, knowing the place beloved by the locals is the ultimate insider one-upmanship. We can trust Sallust as a guide to this sort of lifestyle, and perhaps imagine ourselves in his shoes. One day, if we visit Paris, we might follow in his footsteps and not make any schoolboy errors by taking attractive young women to overly ostentatious restaurants.

In the short story *From A View To A Kill*, published two decades later, Ian Fleming upped the ante on this device even further. In Paris, we learn, Bond doesn't stay in a lesser known but nevertheless expensive hotel like the St Regis: no, he stays in the Terminus Nord, 'because he liked station hotels and because this was the least pretentious and anonymous of them'. And, as in

Wheatley, the restaurants Bond chooses to dine in are never the obvious ones:

> 'For dinner, Bond went to one of the great restaurants—Véfour, the Caneton, Lucas-Carton or the Cochon d'Or. These he considered, whatever Michelin might say about the Tour d'Argent, Maxims and the like, to have somehow avoided the tarnish of the expense account and the dollar.'

This is one of those 'points to comfort and reassure the reader on his journey into fantastic adventure', but it also reveals character. Fleming used 'the real names of things' to show Bond's inner self. *From A View To A Kill* also features a long description of Bond in a Parisian café:

> 'James Bond had his first drink of the evening at Fouquet's. It was not a solid drink. One cannot drink seriously in French cafés. Out of doors on a pavement in the sun is no place for vodka or whisky or gin. A *fine à l'eau* is fairly serious, but it intoxicates without tasting very good. A *quart de champagne* or a *champagne à l'orange* is all right before luncheon, but in the evening one quart leads to another quart and a bottle of indifferent champagne is a bad foundation for the night. Pernod is possible, but it should be drunk in company, and anyway Bond had never liked the stuff because its liquorice taste reminded him of his childhood. No, in cafes you have to drink the least offensive of the musical comedy drinks that go with them, and Bond always had the same thing—an Americano—Bitter Campari, Cinzano, a large slice of lemon peel and soda. For the soda he

always stipulated Perrier, for in his opinion expensive soda water was the cheapest way to improve a poor drink.'

This might appear aimless, but by giving his character forceful, unexpected and intriguing feelings about such an apparently trivial matter as ordering a drink, Fleming brings it to life and puts it centre-stage: this is not a trivial matter to *James Bond*. This, as Fleming put it, is 'the poetry of things'. It's not simply a scene in which a character decides what to drink at a Paris café, but a statement of intent, a philosophy, a weighted moment.

Fleming was not simply interested in brands, but in an attitude towards them. They are sometimes very strong attitudes: Bond knows the best cafés in Paris and knows a lot about drinks, so much so that he's a close-to-insufferable snob about them. He condescends to have a 'musical comedy drink' in a famous Paris bar. He doesn't care what Michelin says about Maxim's—he knows what *he* feels about it, and that's what matters. He doesn't follow the crowd or parrot advertisements and tourist guides, but makes up his own mind about what is the best or most sophisticated option. He has utter faith in his own taste, and as readers we are invited to do the same. Fleming's use of real names and places didn't simply hustle readers past improbabilities in his plots, but established a crucial part of Bond's character: that he is his own man. Bond brands everything around him with his own taste.

The first germs of all this can be seen in *The Scarlet Impostor.*

★

THE NOVEL WAS a turning point for Wheatley, who had been trying for several years to create a hero in the vein of Raffles, Bulldog Drummond and the Saint. Like those three characters, Sallust is a 'bad hat' with vigilante tendencies. But he is also on the right side of the law, a secret agent working in Britain's interests. He has the courage and duty to country of Richard Hannay and the streak of hedonism and decadence of Simon Templar, but a fondness for ungentlemanly behaviour that would have outraged both. Despite the focus on luxury and the nod to Baroness Orczy's Scarlet Pimpernel in its title, *The Scarlet Impostor* has a much more violent tone than most of its antecedents. In this novel, Wheatley introduced Gruppenführer Grauber, who plans to drop our hero into an acid bath; he would become Sallust's arch-enemy as the series progressed. Sallust himself is recognisably the same character as from *Contraband*, a suave, hedonistic, resourceful secret agent, but his brutality is more pronounced:

> 'Before the Nazi could open his mouth Gregory's left hand shot out, caught him by the throat and, swinging him round, forced him back against the wall. With complete ruthlessness Gregory raised his right fist and smashed it into the little man's face.
>
> As his head was jammed against the wall he caught the full force of the blow. A gurgling moan issued from his gaping mouth, but Gregory knew that his own life depended upon putting the wretched man out, and with pitiless persistence he hammered the German's face with his right fist, banging his head against the

wall with each blow until it began to roll about
on his shoulders and Gregory knew that he had
lost consciousness.'

The world was now at war, and this novel was the direct
product of it: Gregory Sallust wasn't in favour of playing
cricket against his enemies any more than his creator.

Wheatley hadn't set out to make Sallust a series
character, but he would prove so popular (several books
in the series sold over a million copies) that he ended up
writing more adventures for him than he'd foreseen. In
doing so, he created a new kind of secret agent character:
as debonair and patriotic as the clubland heroes who had
come before, but significantly more sexually active,
violent and morally ambivalent. Among the first to follow
in the footsteps of *The Scarlet Impostor's* success was his
old friend Peter Cheyney: June 1942 saw the publication
of his novel *Dark Duet*, the first in a new series featuring
a secret unit of sophisticated but brutal British agents who
kill suspected Nazis wherever they find them.

In the next novel in Wheatley's series, *Faked
Passports*, published in June 1940, Sallust travels to the
Arctic Circle. We are given the most complete
description of the character to date, learning that he is in
his late thirties, 'dark, lean-faced' with 'smiling eyes and a
cynical twist to his firm, strong mouth.' After taking a hit
to the back of his head with a spent bullet near Petsamo,
he loses his memory. In and of itself, this is not a
particularly unusual plot device, but amnesia has an
unusual effect on Gregory Sallust, as his girlfriend, the
Countess von Osterberg, reflects:

'In those hectic days they had spent in Munich and Berlin together early in November they had been the most passionate lovers. When they had met again in Helsinki his absence from her had seemed only to have increased his eagerness; but their opportunities for love-making had been lamentably few. Then his injury at Petsamo had changed his mentality in that respect as in all others. On waking on their first morning in the trapper's house he had accepted quite naturally that he was in love with her, but it had been an entirely different kind of love. He was tender and thoughtful for her and followed her every movement with almost dog-like devotion, but he did not seem to know even the first steps in physical love-making any more.

Erika had known the love of many men but to be treated as a saint and placed upon a pedestal was an entirely new experience to her and she had thoroughly enjoyed it. There was something wonderfully refreshing in Gregory's shy, boyish attempts to hold her hand or steal a kiss on the back of her neck when the others were not looking; and she had known that at any moment she chose she could reawake his passions...'

This is strong stuff for a novel published in 1940, with broad hints at both pre-marital sex (the pair would not wed until *They Used Dark Forces*, published in 1964) and promiscuity. But the most striking thing about it is its similarity with the closing scenes of Fleming's *You Only Live Twice*, in which James Bond also loses his memory and in doing so becomes an innocent regarding 'physical love-making'.[41]

The eponymous villain of *The Black Baroness*, published in October 1940, is a middle-aged Frenchwoman with a 'dead white face' and jet-black eyes and hair who acts as 'Hitler's great whore mistress'. Using her position in society, she discovers the types of women senior military figures in Allied and neutral states are attracted to and gives instructions to the Gestapo, who consult their 'list of beautiful harpies' and send the appropriate matches to her; she then sets them to seduce their intended victims. Sallust meets one of these women, Paula von Steinmetz, who naturally tries to seduce him, but he fends her off by pretending he isn't man enough for her:

> '"The sort of man you want is a chap who'd treat you rough and give you a beating if you played him up."
>
> "*Mein Gott, nein!*" Paula protested quickly.
>
> "Oh yes, you do," Gregory assured her. "Every woman does. I don't mean a drunken blackguard or anything of that kind, but a chap with a will of his own who wouldn't stand any nonsense and if he saw you flashing those lovely eyes of yours at anybody else would take you home and give you a good spanking."
>
> Paula's colour deepened a little under her make-up and Gregory knew that he had judged her rightly. She was a strong, highly-sexed young woman who would thoroughly enjoy occasional rows with her lovers and derive tremendous kick from a mild beating-up in which she was finally possessed forcibly, so that her sobs of anger gave way almost imperceptibly to gasps of passionate emotion.

"Well," she admitted slowly, "if one loves a man one naturally expects him to assert himself at times, otherwise how can one possibly respect him?"'

The irony, of course, is that Sallust is precisely the sort of man he is describing, as is made clear elsewhere in the series. This would find an echo in the infamously disturbing passage in *Casino Royale* in which Bond fantasises about Vesper in a very Sallust way:

> 'He felt the bruises on the back of his head and on his right shoulder. He reflected cheerfully how narrowly he had twice that day escaped being murdered. Would he have to sit up all that night and wait for them to come again, or was Le Chiffre even now on his way to Le Havre or Bordeaux to pick up a boat for some corner of the world where he could escape the eyes and the guns of SMERSH?
>
> Bond shrugged his shoulders. Sufficient unto that day had been its evil. He gazed for a moment into the mirror and wondered about Vesper's morals. He wanted her cold and arrogant body. He wanted to see tears and desire in her remote blue eyes and to take the ropes of her black hair in his hands and bend her long body back under his. Bond's eyes narrowed and his face in the mirror looked back at him with hunger.'

Towards the end of *The Black Baroness*, Gregory Sallust meets the baroness herself, who takes the opportunity to poison his wine. Sallust is pinned to his chair, paralysed, and the villain, in the traditional style, calmly discusses his imminent death:

> "'Good-bye, Mr. Sallust; you will die quite
> peacefully and in no great pain.'"

She is proven wrong, naturally: Sallust is rushed to a
doctor and soon recovers. In *From Russia, With Love*,
published in 1957, James Bond would also be poisoned by
an older female villain with a penchant for pimping out
beautiful young women to extract information from the
enemy, although it comes not in a glass of wine but from
a dagger concealed in Rosa Klebb's boot.

After *The Black Baroness*, Wheatley left Sallust again
to write a standalone thriller, *Strange Conflict*, published
in 1941. This, too, seems to have been on Ian Fleming's
radar. It features a privileged group of British and
American agents trying to discover how the Nazis are
predicting the routes of the Atlantic convoys. The trail
leads to Haiti, but before the group even arrive on the
island they are attacked by sharks. They are saved by a
Panama-hatted Haitian called Doctor Saturday, who puts
them up at his house and then takes them to a Voodoo
ceremony, where they witness a sacrifice to Dambala.
Two women wearing black are shooed away by the
priest; one of the group asks Doctor Saturday why:

> 'He replied in his broken French that they were
> in mourning and therefore had no right to
> attend a Dambala ceremony, which was for the
> living. Their association with recent death
> caused them to carry with them, wherever they
> went, the presence of the dreaded Baron
> Samedi.
>
> "Lord Saturday," whispered Marie Lou to the
> Duke. "What a queer name for a god!" But the

Doctor had caught what she had said and turned to smile at her.

"It is another name that they use for Baron Cimeterre. You see, his Holy Day is Saturday. And it is a sort of joke, of which the people never get tired, that my name, too, is Saturday.'"

It is, of course, not a joke at all: Doctor Saturday, they soon discover, is the physical incarnation of Baron Samedi, and the villain they have been trying to track down. In *Live and Let Die*, published 13 years later, Ian Fleming featured a villain with the same name transplanted to Jamaica, where he wrote all his books. In that novel, Samedi is revealed to be a front for a black American gangster known as Mr. Big, as Bond learns from his assistant Solitaire:

> "'You're thinking I shan't understand," he said. "And you're right up to a point. But I know what fear can do to people and I know that fear can be caused by many things. I've read most of the books on Voodoo and I believe that it works. I don't think it would work on me because I stopped being afraid of the dark when I was a child and I'm not a good subject for suggestion or hypnotism. But I know the jargon and you needn't think I shall laugh at it. The scientists and doctors who wrote the books don't laugh at it."
>
> Solitaire smiled. "All right," she said. "Then all I need tell you is that they believe The Big Man is the Zombie of Baron Samedi. Zombies are bad enough by themselves. They're animated corpses that have been made to rise from the

dead and obey the commands of the person who controls them. Baron Samedi is the most dreadful spirit in the whole of Voodooism. He is the spirit of darkness and death. So for Baron Samedi to be in control of his own Zombie is a very dreadful conception. You know what Mr. Big looks like. He is huge and grey and he has great psychic power. It is not difficult for a negro to believe that he is a Zombie and a very bad one at that. The step to Baron Samedi is simple. Mr. Big encourages the idea by having the Baron's fetish at his elbow."'

Mr. Big is exploiting a fear of the supernatural to quell the island's believers, an idea Fleming would re-use in *Dr No* four years later, but this is also the only Bond story to take a leaf out of Wheatley's books and treat the occult as a real force: James Bond believes voodoo works, and we as readers are also asked to accept the supernatural. Solitaire could be mistaken in her belief in Mr. Big's 'great psychic power', but she appears to be genuinely telepathic herself.

V

From Germany, With Love

AFTER ANOTHER SALLUST novel, *V for Vengeance*, Wheatley left the character for a while before returning to him in 1946 for *Come Into My Parlour*. I believe the premise of this book, and the events of three of its chapters, directly inspired *From Russia, With Love*, published 11 years later. It also contains the seeds of James Bond's biography.

Chapter One, titled 'The Spider's Lair', opens with a description of Berlin on the morning of June 23, 1941, introducing us to the status of the war at that date, including the Germans' attitude to it:

> 'For them, to expect victory had now become a habit of mind, and defeat unthinkable.'

After a few paragraphs, we move indoors:

> 'Their confidence was shared by the quiet little middle-aged man who sat at his desk in a

spacious second-floor room that looked out on a sunny courtyard at the back of the great S.S Headquarters on the Alexander Platz.'

Fleming used information from dozens of sources, mixed and distilled through his imagination, when writing *From Russia, With Love*, but one long scene was directly inspired by this chapter. Chapter Four of Fleming's novel, 'The Moguls of Death', begins with a short introduction to SMERSH, 'the official murder organization of the Soviet government'. Then we again move indoors, only this time to SMERSH headquarters at 13 Sretenka Ulitsa in Moscow:

> 'The direction of SMERSH is carried out from the 2nd floor. The most important room on the 2nd floor is a very large light room painted in the pale olive green that is the common denominator of government offices all over the world. Opposite the sound-proofed door, two wide windows look over the courtyard at the back of the building.'

The office's occupant, Colonel General Grubozaboyschikov or 'G', is the head of SMERSH. In both Wheatley and Fleming's scenes, we are introduced to a very senior figure in the hierarchy of the hero's deadliest opponents—the S.S. in Sallust's case, SMERSH in Bond's—as they prepare for an important meeting at enemy headquarters. Cementing that Fleming worked directly from Wheatley's scene, both characters also happen to work in large offices on the second floor that overlook courtyards at the back of their respective buildings.

That isn't in itself all that remarkable, but the pattern of building off Wheatley's structure continues throughout the scene. The inhabitant of the office in *Come Into My Parlour*—who we learn is none other than Heinrich Himmler—now moves into his conference room to hold the monthly meeting of the country's intelligence chiefs:

> 'The three Directors of Intelligence for the Army, Navy and Luftwaffe were present, and the civilian Intelligence Chiefs for the Foreign Office and Economic Warfare. At the far end of the table sat Himmler's Principal Assistant, the S.S. General Kaltenbrunner; the only man, so it was whispered, of whom Himmler himself was afraid. Behind Kaltenbrunner, at a small separate table against the far wall, two S.S. majors waited, unobtrusive but observant, to act as secretaries and take notes of all that passed at the meeting.'

The scene in *From Russia, With Love* also moves to a conference room:

> 'On the far side of the table sat Lieutenant-General Slavin, head of the G.R.U., the intelligence department of the General Staff of the Army, with a full colonel beside him. At the end of the table sat Lieutenant-General Vozdvishensky of R.U.M.I.D., the Intelligence Department of the Ministry of Foreign Affairs, with a middle-aged man in plain clothes. With his back to the door, sat Colonel of State Security Nikitin, Head of Intelligence for the M.G.B., the Soviet Secret Service, with a major at his side.'

In both, we are being shown the senior level of the enemy's spy machinery, and the bland bureaucracy of it becomes increasingly chilling. Wheatley's detail that two S.S. majors sit at a separate table unobtrusively taking notes at the meeting is a wonderfully sinister little touch: it also sounds authoritative, as though Wheatley really knew how these meetings worked. Fleming does much the same, but has each officer in the room accompanied by an A.D.C.:

> 'In the Soviet Union, no man goes alone to a conference. For his own protection, and for the reassurance of his department, he invariably takes a witness so that his department can have independent versions of what went on at the conference and, above all, of what was said on its behalf. This is important in case there is a subsequent investigation. No notes are taken at the conference and decisions are passed back to departments by word of mouth.'

This is even more sinister—'in case there is a subsequent investigation'—but essentially performs the same task: it sounds like Fleming knows how these meetings really take place, and that we're getting an inside look, right inside 'the spider's lair'. And, like Wheatley, he also had an inside source, in his case the Soviet defector Grigori Tokaev.[42]

Wheatley's chapter continues by relating the meeting's progress. Initially it is about the course of the war, but then Himmler comes to an unexpected item on the agenda:

'At item thirteen, he read out: "Gregory Sallust"—paused for a moment, frowned, and added: "What is this? I seem to know that name."

"I had it put on the agenda, Herr Obergruppenführer," said Canaris, quietly.

Himmler squinted at him. "Well, Herr Admiral?"

The Admiral looked round, gathering the attention of his audience. "As you are all aware," he began, "in some respects the British Intelligence Service has deteriorated since the last war. It cannot be denied that they are extremely efficient in securing certain types of information. For example, captured documents prove beyond dispute that their appreciations of our 'Order of Battle' in various theatres of war are uncannily accurate. On the other hand, they seem to have very little idea as to what is going on inside Germany itself. Generally speaking, our internal security is highly satisfactory; but the British do possess a limited number of ace operators who, from time to time, have succeeded in penetrating some of our most closely guarded secrets, and my people tell me that Sallust is the most dangerous of them all."'

Admiral Canaris was the real-life chief of the Abwehr. His raising of Sallust's name is immediately objected to by Gruppenführer Grauber, who registers his surprise that 'the case of any individual enemy agent' would be of sufficient importance to occupy the time 'of such a high-powered meeting as this'. Grauber is fictional, Sallust's arch-enemy from the previous four books. He controls 'the operations of all Gestapo agents in countries outside the Reich', and is liable to pop up anywhere at any time to capture Sallust or one of his allies and sadistically torture them. We haven't seen him previously in a bureaucratic setting like this, and his presence is the equivalent of drawing the camera back to show a new, bigger picture perspective on his run-ins with Sallust.

By openly acknowledging the implausibility of a single agent being so significant as to be discussed by Himmler and other senior Nazi figures, Wheatley hopes to blunt readers' disbelief. He takes this further by having Canaris make the case that Sallust is enough of a threat that he could soon cause their side significant damage:

> "'The progress of our 'K' series of new secret weapons has now reached a point at which their further development necessitates a much greater number of people having knowledge of them. This will automatically increase the danger of the enemy getting wind of these immensely important devices, by which we hope to bring the war with Britain to a successful conclusion without undertaking the hazards of an invasion. If a leak does occur, the British will obviously put their best men on to the job of securing for them the secrets of Peenemünde. Sallust speaks German as well as if he was born here, so all the odds are that he will be allocated to this task. Prevention being better than cure, I should like to have the Herr Gruppenführer's assurance that adequate precautions are being taken against him.'"

The pattern of this is repeated in Fleming's novel. The Russians also discuss the progress of the war—the Cold one—with references to events in Morocco, Yugoslavia,

Cyprus and elsewhere. They speak rather more highly of the British than the Germans do, and their meeting doesn't have any points on the agenda other than Bond, but scepticism over the importance of the single enemy agent under discussion is similarly expressed:

> "'Within the Secret Service, this man may be a local hero or he may not. It will depend on his appearance and personal characteristics. Of these I know nothing. He may be fat and greasy and unpleasant. No one makes a hero out of such a man, however successful he is."

This doubt is immediately countered:

> Nikitin broke in. "English spies we have captured speak highly of this man. He is certainly much admired in his Service. He is said to be a lone wolf, but a good looking one.'"

In *Come Into My Parlour*, Himmler checks Canaris' analysis of the threat by asking Grauber what he knows of the British agent:

> 'Grauber shrugged his great shoulders. "The Herr Admiral exaggerates the danger. Sallust is certainly a man to watch. He is resolute and resourceful, and he has pulled off some very clever coups. So far he has always managed to elude us; but if he puts his nose inside Germany again, I'll get him."

Even monstrous Gestapo chiefs can have their turf unexpectedly invaded by other departments. Grauber's response to the pressure is to airily talk down the idea that this single British agent is a major threat, while at the same making it clear that he is a danger. In doing so, he is defending his department and trying to evade personal blame for having failed to stop Sallust. His underplaying of Sallust's impact is in itself suggestive of his effectiveness, as he can't afford to pretend that he's no threat at all—the best he can do is admit he has proven to be a menace in the past, but not so notable one that a whole operation proposed by another agency need be devoted to catching him. The act might be enough to fool the others in the room, but for readers of the series to date there's a pleasing irony: implausible as it might seem that Himmler and other senior Nazis would have discussed a single agent in a meeting such as this, we know that Canaris' assessment was the right one: Sallust is in fact capable of changing the fate of world events, and Grauber having to pretend otherwise considering their history is rather delicious. By having his fictional arch-villain interact with real-life senior Nazis like Canaris and Himmler, and doing so in a closely detailed and seemingly authentic setting, Wheatley is also deepening the stakes of the series so far. The evil Grauber is himself under pressure from men we know to be even more evil. At the same time, Wheatley is making Sallust a more credible figure: the real-life head of the Abwehr knows his name, and will set in motion the plot of the novel.

Fleming does something very similar in his scene. General Vozdvishensky defends having initially failed to recall the agent under discussion:

> "'Certainly I know the name of this Bond. He has been a great trouble to us at different times.

> But today my mind is full of other names—
> names of people who are causing us trouble
> today, this week. I am interested in football, but
> I cannot remember the name of every foreigner
> who has scored a goal against the Dynamos.'"

Vozdvishensky is the (fictional) head of Soviet foreign intelligence efforts. He is a new character to the series, so there is not nearly as much irony in his assessment of Bond, but Fleming is using the jostling for position among the enemy's spy chiefs in a very similar way to Wheatley, to give a higher level view of the novels to date by showing how they have been viewed by senior intelligence figures. Like Grauber, Vozdvishensky responds to pressure from his colleagues by denying the single British agent is a major threat, but as readers we know he is.

The irony of Grauber being forced to claim that Gregory Sallust isn't too much of a problem would have been lost on new readers to the series. Wheatley was conscious of this. To bring them up to speed on the context, he has Canaris rattle off a few examples of his hero's activities:

> "'He even had the effrontery to beard
> Reichsmarschall Goering at Karinhall, and got
> away with it; and I have good reason to believe
> that he completely fooled von Geisenheim, one
> of our astutest Generals, less than a month ago
> in Paris.'"

The first incident appeared in *Faked Passports*, the second in *V for Vengeance*.

Similarly, Fleming uses the bickering intelligence chiefs to give us a potted history of Bond's previous exploits:

> "'Comrade Colonel Nikitin will no doubt refresh our memories further, but I recall that this Bond has at lease twice frustrated the operations of SMERSH. That is,' he added, 'before I assumed control of the department. There was this affair in France, at that Casino town. The man Le Chiffre. An excellent leader of the Party in France. He foolishly got into some money troubles. But he would have got out of them if this Bond had not interfered. I recall that the Department had to act quickly and liquidate the Frenchman. The executioner should have dealt with the Englishman at the same time, but he did not. Then there was this Negro of ours in Harlem. A great man—one of the greatest foreign agents we have ever employed, and with a vast network behind him. There was some business about a treasure in the Caribbean. I forget the details. This Englishman was sent out by the Secret Service and smashed the whole organization and killed our man. It was a great reverse. Once again my predecessor should have proceeded ruthlessly against this English spy."
>
> Colonel Nikitin broke in. "We had a similar experience in the case of the German, Drax, and the rocket. You will recall the matter, Comrade General. A most important *konspiratsia*. The General Staff were deeply involved. It was a matter of High Policy which could have borne decisive fruit. But again it was this Bond who frustrated the operation. The

German was killed. There were grave consequences for the State. There followed a period of serious embarrassment which was only solved with difficulty.'"

Here we have the action of *Casino Royale, Live and Let Die* and *Moonraker* summarised from the perspective of senior figures in SMERSH. (The only novel in the series to date whose events are not mentioned is *Diamonds are Forever*, which had no connection to Cold War espionage.)

In both novels, the scenes develop the idea that the hero of the series is a worthwhile target to be the focus of the attention of the chief enemy's most senior figures. Wheatley concludes his chapter with Himmler rapping out his verdict:

> "'If this man is so dangerous he must be eliminated before he has a chance to do us any further mischief. Lure him here. Set a trap for him and kill him. See to that, Grauber, or I will make you answer for it personally. Within three months, I require a certificate of Sallust's death from you.'"

One can almost follow Ian Fleming's thought process as he read these lines. The idea of Grauber having to not only kill Sallust but also provide his death certificate is wonderfully menacing, but Fleming thought of a way to better it:

> 'General G.'s hand went to the internal office telephone. He spoke to his A.D.C. "Death Warrant," he said harshly. "Made out in the name of 'James Bond'".

The scene ends with the men at the table passing around Bond's death warrant, each of them signing it in turn, after which we are introduced to Rosa Klebb.

There are, naturally, thousands of differences between these long scenes, but their structure and tone are strikingly similar, and the core premise the same in both: the leaders of the enemy camp hold a meeting at their headquarters, snipe at each other, but eventually agree to set a trap and kill Britain's greatest secret agent. Both scenes set up the main plot of the novels. In Wheatley's, the Germans predict that the agent in question will be sent to find out about their new 'K' series of weapons. SMERSH's *konspiratsia* adds a sweetener to the British to make sure Bond is sent—Tatiana's supposed adoration of him—but the main lure is also a piece of top-secret technology, the Spektor cipher machine. Both plots also involve the manipulation of a beautiful woman, albeit in different ways.

But this is not the end of *Come Into My Parlour's* influence on Fleming. He also drew on it for another of his novels, and in a way that goes to the heart of James Bond's identity. In the chapter following the meeting at S.S. Headquarters, Grauber approaches Canaris to ask his advice on trapping Sallust, asking if he has any further details about the man. Canaris' response is worth quoting at length:

> "'Sallust comes of good middle-class stock, but his parents were only moderately well off and both of them died when he was quite young. He was an imaginative and therefore troublesome boy and after only two and a half terms was expelled for innumerable breaches of

discipline from his public school, Dulwich College. With the idea of taming him, his uncle sent him as a cadet to H.M.S. Worcester. The freer life seems to have suited him, but again, owing to his refractory nature, he was never made a Petty Officer, as they term their Prefects. On leaving he did not go to sea, because he did not consider that such a career offered a sufficiently remunerative future: instead he used a portion of his patrimony to give himself a year on the Continent. He has a quite exceptional flair for languages so he could soon speak German and French like a native. He was still at an age when he ought to have been at school, but he was already his own master and a handsome, precocious young blackguard. The women adored him and he had an insatiable curiosity about the night life, both high and low, of all the cities he visited, so there wasn't much he hadn't done by the time the war broke out and he returned to England."

Canaris paused for a moment, then went on: "He got a commission at once in a Territorial Field Artillery Regiment, and in due course was sent to France. At the age of twenty-one he was serving on the staff of the Third Army. At the battle of Cambrai he was wounded and carries the scar to this day. It lifts the outer corner of his left eyebrow, giving him a slightly satanic appearance. He showed great gallantry at the time he was wounded and was given the M.C.

"After the War he took up journalism; not regular work, but unusual assignments that took him abroad again. As a special correspondent he saw the high spots of the Graeco-Turkish war of nineteen nineteen, and the Russo-Polish war of nineteen twenty. Then he spent a lot of time in Central Europe, studying the development of the new states that emerged from the Versailles and Trianon Treaties—Hungary, Czechoslovakia, and so on. It was through his articles on such subjects, I believe, that he came into touch with that formidable old rascal Sir Pellinore Gwaine-Cust."

Grauber's solitary eye flickered slightly and he suddenly sat forward. "So you know about him, do you? My compliments, Herr Admiral; he keeps himself so much in the background that I thought hardly anyone here had the least idea of the power he wields behind the scenes on every major problem concerning the British Empire."

"Oh, yes, I know about him." The Admiral's thin mouth twisted into a cynical smile. "He took seven thousand marks off me at baccarat one night at Deauville in nineteen twenty four, drank me under the table afterwards and sent the money back next morning with a charming little note to the effect that, seeing the poor state of Germany's post-war finances, he did not feel it fair to take such a sum off one of her secret agents at a single sitting. You can repeat that story if you like. I have often related it as a lesson in good manners to my subordinates...'"

Fleming and Wheatley both added a great deal of their own tastes and experiences to their characters (Wheatley was wounded at Cambrai), and fictional secret agents tended to be good-looking, fluent in languages, with extensive combat experience. But the similarities between the biography of Sallust presented here and that given for Bond in his obituary in *You Only Live Twice*, published in 1964, go far beyond the conventions of the genre, or coincidence:

'James Bond was born of a Scottish father, Andrew Bond of Glencoe, and a Swiss mother, Monique Delacroix, from the Canton de Vaud. His father being a foreign representative of the Vickers armaments firm, his early education, from which he inherited a first-class command of French and German, was entirely abroad. When he was eleven years of age, both his parents were killed in a climbing accident in the Aiguilles Rouges above Chamonix, and the youth came under the guardianship of an aunt, since deceased, Miss Charmian Bond, and went to live with her at the quaintly-named hamlet of Pett Bottom near Canterbury in Kent. There, in a small cottage hard by the attractive Duck Inn, his aunt, who must have been a most erudite and accomplished lady, completed his education for an English public school, and, at the age of twelve or thereabouts, he passed satisfactorily into Eton, for which College he had been entered at birth by his father. It must be admitted that his career at Eton was brief and undistinguished and, after only two halves, as a result, it pains me to record, of some alleged trouble with one of the boys' maids, his aunt was requested to remove him. She managed to obtain his transfer to Fettes, his father's old school. Here the atmosphere was somewhat Calvinistic, and both academic and athletic standards were rigorous. Nevertheless, though inclined to be solitary by nature, he established some firm friendships among the traditionally famous athletic circles at the school. By the time he left, at the early age of seventeen, he had twice fought for the school as a light-weight and had, in addition, founded the first serious judo class at a British public school. By now it was 1941 and, by claiming an age of nineteen and with the help of an old Vickers colleague of his father, he entered a branch of what was subsequently to become the Ministry of Defence. To serve the confidential nature of his duties, he was accorded the rank of lieutenant in the Special Branch of the R.N.V.R., and it is a measure of the satisfaction his services gave to his superiors that he ended the war with the rank of Commander...'

To summarize: James Bond and Gregory Sallust both lost both their parents at a young age; Fleming specifies at what age and how it happened. Both were sent to public school (the same one as their respective authors), but expelled after similarly short amounts of time. As terms at Eton are known as 'halves', this may be why Bond did not last quite as long as Sallust: 'two and a half halves' wouldn't have worked. Wheatley was himself expelled from Dulwich, whereas Fleming lasted the duration at Eton.

Both Bond and Sallust had naval training while young, although Bond's is significantly more extensive. Wheatley based his character's experience on his own: he had also been a cadet on HMS Worcester. Bond ends the war a Commander in the Royal Navy Volunteer Reserve, as did Fleming. (In *Traitors' Gate*, published in 1958, Sallust would become a Wing Commander in the Royal Air Force Volunteer Reserve, which was Wheatley's rank by the end of the war.) Both Bond and Sallust have fluent German and French. Both discovered the attentions of women at a young age, Sallust while roaming the cities of Europe and Bond a little earlier with the maid incident. Both are decorated: Sallust an M.C. and Bond a C.M.G.

Then there is Canaris' anecdote about losing money to Sir Pellinore at baccarat in Deauville in 1924. This is very reminiscent of the incident that Fleming claimed, in an interview with *Playboy*, had inspired *Casino Royale*:

> 'I was on my way to America with the Director of Naval Intelligence, Admiral Godfrey. We were in Estoril in Portugal, and while we were waiting for transport, we killed some time in the casino. While there, I recognised some German agents, and I thought it would be a brilliant coup to play with them, break them, take their money. Instead, of course, they took mine. Most embarrassing. This incident appears in *Casino Royale*, my first book—but, of course, Bond does not lose.'[43]

Fleming told several versions of this story, but a British operative's attempt to deliver a blow to Germany's fortunes in a foreign casino is the 'hook' of the anecdote in all its forms, and it's a strikingly unusual idea. So what happened here? In *Casino Royale*, Fleming changed the location of Estoril to Royale-les-Eaux, a fictionalised version of Deauville, and baccarat was also the game played. It seems unlikely, therefore, that Fleming had told Wheatley about the incident, as they would have then both to have independently decided to relocate it to northern France, with Wheatley doing so first. So perhaps it was the other way around: Wheatley had heard of such an incident happening and told the anecdote to Fleming, who then decided to try it out himself while in Estoril, after which he used it in the plot of *Casino Royale*.

★

Come Into My Parlour was an unusually violent novel for 1946. Erika falls into the clutches of Grauber, who forces her to watch a woman being tortured with electrodes. After escaping from the Lubyanka and the bowels of a U-boat, Sallust infiltrates the *Schloss* in which Erika is being held and follows Helga, a vivacious Gestapo gaoler with 'good legs and provocative breasts' to her room, where she strips off her fur coat for him. He shoots her in the back, but the bullet goes through her spine in the area of her kidneys and doesn't kill her outright. Reasoning that the lower part of her body is the life of such an 'over-sexed young animal', Sallust doesn't hesitate:

> 'He knew what he would have wished himself had he been her. Putting the point of his gun within a few inches of the base of her skull he blew out her brains. He felt no compunction at all about the act. It was the merciful thing to do.'

Four more Sallust novels followed, the final adventure in the series, *The White Witch of The South Seas*, being published in 1968. Wheatley outlived Fleming, but doesn't seem to have ever publicly mentioned that his work was an influence on James Bond. This might be because to have done so would have detracted from his sense of his own achievements. Wheatley often blew his own trumpet—sometimes even within the pages of his own novels—but having sustained millions of sales over several decades, he would have had reason to believe his characters would be regarded by subsequent generations in much the same way as the Scarlet Pimpernel, the Three Musketeers and Richard Hannay. But his star quickly faded, and he is all but forgotten now. His books soon dated in part because of his politics: although he could throw in some unexpected perspectives, he was for the most part an unabashed reactionary imperialist who made Fleming look like Jeremy Corbyn. He had always felt that other writers had trapped themselves by focussing on just one character, so had alternated his series, and genres; but this strategy seems to have backfired, as he has not been remembered for one character the way Fleming is for James Bond. Indeed, his spy novels are barely remembered at all. There were successful film adaptations of Wheatley's work, but none captured the public's imagination to anything like the same degree as the Bond films. None of the Sallust books were ever adapted for film, Wheatley thought in part because the necessity of vast crowds and battle-scenes would have made them too expensive to produce.[44]

It could also be that Wheatley was unaware of the extent to which he had influenced Fleming. In his memoirs, he mentioned that he had been friends with Fleming, but didn't elaborate on it. But he was well aware of Fleming's success. In his novel *The Unholy Crusade*, published in 1967, he even referred to himself in the same sentence as Fleming, who had died three years earlier. His hero, aspiring novelist Adam Gordon, visits his cynical publisher, from whom he learns the hard facts of a writer's life:

> 'He must not be misled by the incomes made by such writers as Agatha Christie, Somerset Maugham, Dennis Wheatley, Ian Fleming, J.B. Priestley, A.J. Cronin, Howard Spring and a few others of that kind. They could be counted on the fingers of two hands.'

This is a classic piece of self-advertising from Wheatley, although there's a touch of desperation to it, almost as if he is reminding himself as well as his readers that he is in the same league as the others. Later in the same book, he makes a bid for establishing himself as one of the thriller greats, when he has a Wing Commander marvel at his hero's adventures:

> '"So you are now Richard Hannay, Gregory Sallust and Uncle Tom Cobley and all." His face suddenly became serious. "But this is a dangerous game you're playing, and your pals in the Mexican Security set-up won't equip you against all emergencies. I mean, real secret agents don't have daggers that spring out of the soles of their shoes, cars that eject flame and tintacks in the path of their pursuers, and all those other silly, amusing gadgets that one reads about in the Bond books."'

A few paragraphs later, this character warns our hero that if his enemies realize what he is planning to do he may find a knife stuck into him faster than he can 'take the first sip of a dry Martini'. Wheatley is going to some lengths to position Gregory Sallust as having followed in the line of Buchan's hero. At the same time, he appears to be belittling Bond, who is not just heroically intrepid like Hannay and Sallust, but completely unrealistic to boot.

Or perhaps not, as most of the 'silly, amusing gadgets' in Fleming's work were inspired by real devices, something that Wheatley, with his experiences in the war, might well have known.[45]

However, Wheatley doesn't seem to have known James Bond all that well: 007 drinks *vodka* martini, of course. This chimes with research done by Phil Baker: according to an exhaustive catalogue Wheatley made of his 4,000-strong library in 1964 for insurance and tax purposes, he didn't own any of Fleming's books.[46] Nevertheless, he did comment directly on Fleming's work on at least one occasion. In 1971, Swedish thriller expert Iwan Morelius asked Wheatley what he thought of James Bond. 'I enjoyed Ian Fleming's books,' he replied, 'particularly the first, *Casino Royale*, which I thought was his best, but some of the others such as the one about the Chinese doctor in the Caribbean were, I thought, so improbable as, to my mind, he was written out.'[47]

This seems a peculiar remark coming from Wheatley, whose plots were often extremely improbable, but perhaps he felt that Fleming's strengths lay more in traditional spy thriller territory: *Casino Royale* was certainly much more low-key than *Dr No*.

It might also be that Wheatley *was* aware of his influence on Fleming, but didn't think it particularly remarkable. Fleming took some elements of his work, but dramatically refashioned them into something entirely new. One could call it derivative, but Wheatley was himself a highly derivative writer: Gregory Sallust was built on the shoulders of Bulldog Drummond and the Saint. He added fresh twists to them, and Fleming did the same to Sallust. In his memoirs, Wheatley remarked of his

1938 novel *The Golden Spaniard* that 'the main theme was a plagiarism of Alexandre Dumas' *Twenty Years After*', before commenting that he felt it was one of the best books he had written.[48]

Fleming also never acknowledged Wheatley's influence on his work, but that's hardly surprising. He acknowledged the influence of John Buchan, E Phillips Oppenheim, Sax Rohmer and Sapper, but these were all writers long past their heyday and comparisons between his work and theirs didn't show him up as being derivative, simply because he didn't draw as much from them. Hammett and Chandler were writing crime fiction in another vernacular: nobody could think they were too close, and an association with their work made his seem up-to-date. Wheatley, on the other hand, was still writing spy thrillers, and drawing attention to his influence might have been revealing a little too much of what went into making the Bond 'sausage'. Fleming was also notably naïve about the perils of using others' ideas as a springboard for his own work; his use of George Griffith's *The Outlaws of The Air* in *Thunderball* went unnoticed in the storm of accusations of plagiarism and legal proceedings over that novel, which producer Kevin McClory claimed was too similar to a script he and others had worked on prior to its publication. Fleming settled out of court.

But then how has Wheatley's influence been so overlooked by Fleming's critics? It's no coincidence that Kingsley Amis, O.F. Snelling and others hopped from the clubland heroes to Bond, leaving a gap of three or four decades between—they had read the former in boyhood and moved on to other fare as adults before being drawn back into the genre by Fleming's huge success and new spin on it. Sometimes the coincidences of personal taste left gaps that were never filled in. Snelling skipped over Leslie Charteris as a potentially significant influence on Fleming in two sentences because he didn't personally find The Saint a memorable character, while Julian Symons claimed that a 'characteristic Wheatley book contains chunks of pre-digested history served up in a form which may appeal to readers with a mental age of twelve'.[49] That's a little harsh, I think, but then I wasn't much older when I first devoured the Sallust novels, and of course millions of teenagers have read James Bond stories. It's no great surprise when later in the same book Symons claims:

> 'Fleming is the heir of Buchan and 'Sapper', and James Bond was a more sophisticated version of Bulldog Drummond.'[50]

This is a view that has solidified over the decades, but which, I hope I've shown, is far too bald. But neither am I saying that Wheatley was Fleming's only influence. As well as his own experiences and fertile imagination, he drew on a large and disparate body of material when writing his novels: it was the way in which he collated it all that created their magic. So he might take a dose of authoritative-sounding facts from E.H. Cookridge's *Soviet Spy Net*, snippets of inside information on life in Berlin from *Sunday Times* correspondent Antony Terry, testimony from a Soviet defector, add a plot premise and the structure of a couple of chapters from Wheatley's *Come Into My Parlour*, throw in his own observations of the international situation, and fashion from it all a rich but distinctive stew. One testament to Fleming's originality is that his voice is so unmistakeable—wherever the ideas came from, he transformed them into something else entirely.

Fleming also outgrew Wheatley's influence, and those of writers like Buchan and Sapper. Even as early as *Moonraker*, we find an ending that subverts the genre's expectations, and James Bond adopts a pose that is much more self-reflective than Gregory Sallust could ever have managed:

> "'I'm going to marry that man," she said quietly. "Tomorrow afternoon." And then, as if no other explanation was needed, "His name's Detective-Inspector Vivian."
>
> "Oh," said Bond. He smiled stiffly. "I see."
>
> There was a moment of silence during which their eyes slid away from each other.
>
> And yet why should he have expected anything else? A kiss. The contact of two frightened bodies clinging together in the midst of danger. There had been nothing more. And there had been the engagement ring to tell him. Why had he automatically assumed that it had only been worn to keep Drax at bay? Why had he imagined that she shared his desires, his plans?
>
> And now what? wondered Bond. He shrugged his shoulders to shift the pain of failure-the pain of failure that is so much greater than the pleasure of success. The exit line. He must get out of these two young lives and take his cold heart elsewhere. There must be no regrets. No false sentiment. He must play the role which she expected of him. The tough man of the

world. The Secret Agent. The man who was only a silhouette.'

As his career progressed, Fleming strained at the shackles of the genre even further, eventually writing short stories that owed more to Graham Greene and Somerset Maugham. And while Wheatley and Fleming's tone, plots, characters and even world views were often very similar, their style and pace weren't. The Sallust series is about a secret agent on the run, usually behind enemy lines, constantly in physical danger and managing to survive by the skin of his teeth. He is also constantly changing into uniforms to impersonate Nazi officers and other figures, and these aspects of his work helped pave the way for the likes of Alistair Maclean's *Where Eagles Dare* and Adam Hall's Quiller novels.

In contrast, Fleming removed pace almost entirely from his thrillers, concentrating instead on the excitement of the various elements: the outlandish villain, the beautiful girl, the extraordinary conspiracy, all pulled together by his unique voice and filtered through the eyes of James Bond. Wheatley used incidental atmospheric details to make his peripatetic plots more realistic; Fleming used peripatetic plots as diversions to showcase the main action of his novels, which *was* the atmospheric details.

But despite these differences, there can be little doubt that Wheatley's novels were a lodestar for Fleming, and the seeds of both the character of James Bond and of many of his adventures are contained within them. Bond shares attributes with Bulldog Drummond, Richard Hannay, The Saint and other characters, but they pale in comparison to the similarities with Gregory Sallust. Sallust is Britain's greatest secret agent, dark-haired and cruelly handsome, has a facial scar, was orphaned at a young age, was expelled from his public school, has a naval background, falls in love with and eventually marries a Countess, but is also a womanizer, is fluent in French and German, a daredevil, ruthless and yet frequently sentimental, well-informed, fond of gambling, Champagne and Savile Row suits. James Bond is every single one of these. In addition, Fleming was clearly inspired by the Sallust novels for several key plot ideas. It's time to classify Dennis Wheatley as a major influence on Ian Fleming.

Acknowledgements

With many thanks to: Ihsan Amanatullah, Phil Baker, Ajay Chowdhury, and the late Iwan Morelius.

Did you enjoy this book? If so, you might also like some of these titles by Jeremy Duns:

Agent of Influence

Antony Terry and the Shaping of Cold War Fact and Fiction

He was a giant of Cold War journalism, reporting from the alleyways of Vienna, Berlin and Budapest and the jungles of Biafra and Paraguay. A war hero, a Nazi-hunter, a spy and a master manipulator, he was also a major influence on several of the 20th century's greatest thriller-writers. Jeremy Duns delves into the many worlds of Antony Terry.

Available in paperback and ebook editions from Amazon worldwide.

Rogue Royale

The Lost Bond Film by the 'Shakespeare of Hollywood'

In the mid-Sixties, the James Bond films became a global phenomenon as the world thrilled to their spectacular action sequences and cool gadgets. But the films nearly went in a very different direction, with a much darker treatment of Ian Fleming's first novel by Hollywood's most acclaimed screenwriter. In *Rogue Royale*, journalist and spy novelist Jeremy Duns unearths Ben Hecht's drafts of *Casino Royale*.

Available in paperback and ebook editions from Amazon worldwide.

Diamonds in the Rough
Investigations into the Worlds of Ian Fleming and James Bond

So much has been written about James Bond that it seems scarcely imaginable there is any more territory to mine. But in *Diamonds In The Rough*, Jeremy Duns shares the fruits of several years of research into unexplored aspects of Ian Fleming and his universe, from lost novels and screenplays to hidden inspirations. This book collects six articles previously published in *The Sunday Times*, *The Sunday Telegraph* and elsewhere.

Available in paperback and ebook editions from Amazon worldwide.

Duns on Bond

An omnibus edition featuring *Rogue Royale* and *Diamonds in the Rough*. Available in paperback and ebook editions from Amazon worldwide.

Dead Drop
The True Story of Oleg Penkovsky and the Cold War's Most Dangerous Operation

In August 1960, a Soviet colonel called Oleg Penkovsky tried to make contact with the West. His first attempt was to approach two American students in Moscow. He handed them a bulky envelope and pleaded with them to deliver it to the American embassy. Inside was an offer to work as a 'soldier-warrior' for the free world.

MI6 and the CIA ran Penkovsky jointly, in an operation that ran through the showdown over Berlin and the Cuban Missile Crisis. He provided crucial intelligence, including photographs of rocket manuals that helped Kennedy end the Cuba crisis and avert a war. Codenamed HERO, Penkovsky is widely seen as the most important spy of the Cold War, and the CIA–MI6 operation, run as the world stood on the brink of nuclear destruction, has never been bettered.

But how exactly did the Russians detect Penkovsky, and why did they let him continue his contact with his handlers for months afterwards? Could it be that the whole Cuban Missile Crisis was part of a Soviet deception operation—and has another betrayal hidden in plain sight all these years? Thrilling, evocative and hugely controversial, *Dead Drop* blows apart the myths surrounding one of the Cold War's greatest spy operations.

Available in paperback and ebook editions from booksellers worldwide.

Tradecraft
Collected Journalism on Spy Fact and Fiction

Tradecraft is a collection of 20 articles about spy fact and fiction. Featuring articles previously published in *The Sunday Times, The Guardian, The Daily Telegraph, Time Out* and elsewhere, as well as previously unpublished material, *Tradecraft* will take you on a journey through the espionage world that will leave you shaken—and perhaps a little stirred.

Available in paperback and ebook editions from Amazon worldwide.

The Dark Novels

The acclaimed Cold War spy series featuring anti-hero agent Paul Dark:

Free Agent
Song of Treason
The Moscow Option
Spy Out The Land

Available in paperback and ebook editions from booksellers worldwide.

Source Notes

[1] 'What Became of Harting?' by Richard Boston, *New York Times*, 27 October 1968 (a review of John le Carre's *A Small Town In Germany*); *The Oxford Companion to English Literature*, edited by Margaret Drabble (Oxford University Press, 2006), p963.

[2] *The Devil Is A Gentleman* by Phil Baker (Dedalus, 2009), p413.

[3] *The Time Has Come* by Dennis Wheatley (Arrow, 1981), p662.

[4] 'The Man Who Can't Help Hitting The Jackpot' by Martin Fox, *The Daily Mail*, 30 August 1966, as cited in *The Devil Is A Gentleman*, p640.

[5] Many of the papers he wrote during the war were collected in his book *Stranger Than Fiction* (The Anchor Press, 1959).

[6] *The Deception Planners: My Secret War* by Dennis Wheatley (Hutchinson, 1980), p41.

[7] Ibid., p154.

[8] Ibid., pp151-153 and pp191-193.

[9] *Peter Fleming: A Biography* by Duff Hart-Davis (Oxford University Press, 1987), pp271-274.

[10] *The Deception Planners*, p98.

[11] *The Devil is a Gentleman*, p420.

[12] *The Deception Planners*, pp36-37

[13] Phil Baker to author, 18 April 2007. Also see *Ian Fleming* by Andrew Lycett (Phoenix, 1996), p134, which mentions Wheatley was 'an occasional dinner guest' of Ian Fleming.

[14] Lycett, pp151-152.

[15] *Her Majesty's Secret Service* by Christopher Andrew (Penguin, 1987), p334.

[16] See *The Life of Ian Fleming* by John Pearson (The Companion Book Club, 1966), pp117-118. For more on McCormick's deceptions, see my article 'Licence

to Hoax' in *Tradecraft* (Skerry, 2016). Writers who have repeated McCormick's fabrication about Hess include Anthony Masters in his 1984 biography of Knight, in which he claimed without any evidence that Fleming was 'fascinated' by Knight and modelled 'M' in part on him. See *The Man Who Was M* (Grafton, 1986), p157.

[17] Driberg introducing Wheatley to Crowley: *The Time Has Come*, pp605-607; M/8: *M: Maxwell Knight, MI5's Greatest Spymaster* by Henry Hemming (Preface Digital, 2017), loc3397; Driberg's career as a Soviet agent of influence: *The Mitrokhin Archive* (Basic Books, 1999), pp400-403. In the late 1930s, Wheatley was 'inclined towards' Mussolini's fascism, but throughout his life was friends with figures from all walks of life and across the political spectrum – he was anything if predictable. When a friend brought William 'Lord Haw Haw' Joyce to one of his parties, Wheatley was amused to hear Joyce's claim that Hermann Goering was a fan of his novels – and his inclusion of a long scene with Goering in one of his novels might be have been a result of this. But he was also already aware of the Nazis' persecution of the Jews and others, and was unimpressed by Joyce otherwise. See *The Time Has Come*, pp640-641.

[18] The quote is from *The Life of Ian Fleming* by Pearson, p140. Andrew Lycett also gives an account of a typical Fleming evening, which includes him reading a volume of poetry, a copy of the *New Yorker* and 'latest U.S. thriller' at Boodle's; Lycett, p261.

[19] 'The Exclusive Bond: Mr Fleming on his hero', letter from Fleming, *The Manchester Guardian*, 5 April 1958, p4.

[20] *Counterpoint* by Roy Newquist (Rand McNally & Company, 1964), pp211-212.

[21] 'The Tragic Spy' by Ian Fleming, *Sunday Times*, 17 November 1957, p8.

[22] *The Spy's Bedside Book*, edited by Graham and Hugh Greene (The New English Library, 1957), p37.

[23] Script for 'Tempo' programme on Fleming and Bond, broadcast on I.T.V. on 14 October 1962, 14.25. My thanks to Philip Purser for the copy of his original script.

[24] See http://www.denniswheatley.info/sams_books/misc6.htm

[25] Pearson, p207.

[26] Hutchinson advert for *Contraband* in *The Observer*, 6 November 1936, p7.

[27] Hodder & Stoughton advertisement for *The Oldest Road* by D.G. Waring, featuring Wheatley's praise of it, *The Observer*, 28 August 1938, p4. For Waring/Harnett and The Link, see *Fellow Travellers of the Right: British Enthusiasts for Nazi Germany, 1933-1939* by Richard Griffiths (Faber Finds, 2015), location 6513. It seems likely Wheatley was introduced to her via Maxwell Knight, who between 1924 and 1927 had been Director of Intelligence for the British Fascists, before turning poacher on them. See *The Devil Is A Gentleman*,

p351.

[28] *The Devil Is a Gentleman*, p344.

[29] Ibid., p345.

[30] Pearson, p211.

[31] The previous edition of this book stated in error that Menzies was head of M.I.6; he did become 'C', but in November 1939, following the death of Hugh Sinclair.

[32] Unsigned letter marked 'Stottinger' (her maiden name), 16 June, 1938, UK National Archives, KV 2/1280; and memo signed B.5b (Knight's section), 20 May, 1938, ibid.

[33] Wheatley to F.W. Leggett, 10 January 1939, UK National Archives, KV 2/1280. She looks to have been employed by him until at least January 1943: a letter from Inspector Hamilton Miller of Edinburgh City Police that month says Gaertner is 'described as a Translator and Research Worker for Mr Denis [sic] Wheatley, 8 St. John's Wood Park, London, N.W.8.', UK National Archives, KV 2/1277.

[34] Knight to Wheatley, 11 January 1939, UK National Archives, KV 2/1280.

[35] *The Time Has Come*, pp641-642; *The Devil Is A Gentleman*, pp401-402.

[36] Hutchinson advertisement featuring this line in *The Observer*, 24 September 1939, p4.

[37] See Wheatley's inscription in his copy of the book, available at http://www.denniswheatley.info/museum/room.asp?id=7&exhib=18

[38] Obituary of Knight in *Growing Point*, Volume 6, 1968, p1092.

[39] *How To Write A Thriller* by Ian Fleming, *Show*, August 1962.

[40] Ibid.

[41] For a fuller analysis of this, and its similarities with another thriller, see my article 'Bourne Yesterday' in *Diamonds In The Rough* (Skerry, 2014).

[42] *Historical Dictionary of Ian Fleming's World of Intelligence* by Nigel West (The Scarecrow Press, 2009), pp220-221; and see Fleming's inscription in his author's copy of the novel: http://www.indiana.edu/~liblilly/etexts/fleming/index.shtml#IF03133

[43] Interview with Fleming, *Playboy*, December 1964, p104.

[44] *Fyra decennier med Dennis Wheatley* by Iwan Hedman (Morelius) and Jan Alexandersson (DAST, 1973), p177.

[45] The spikes Le Chiffre uses against Bond's Bentley in *Casino Royale* are assumed by Bond to be 'an adaptation of the nail-studded devices used by the Resistance against German staff-cars'. Britain's Special Operations Executive also had a device called the Tyreburster, a charge that was to be 'placed on the road or in ground where vehicles are likely to move'. See *Secret Agent's Handbook*, introduced by Roderick Bailey (Max Press, 2008), p42. The book is derived from Descriptive Catalogue of Special Devices and Supplies, 1944, UK National Archives, HS

7/28. S.O.E. didn't create a shoe with a dagger, but did have an incendiary attaché case very much like the one used by Bond in *From Russia, With Love*; ibid., p121.

[46] Phil Baker to author, 19 April, 2007.

[47] *Fyra decennier med Dennis Wheatley*, p176.

[48] *The Time Has Come*, p628.

[49] *Bloody Murder: From the Detective Story to the Crime Novel* by Julian Symons (Viking, 1985 revised edition), p202.

[50] Ibid., p223.

Printed by Amazon Italia Logistica S.r.l.
Torrazza Piemonte (TO), Italy

11328835R00057